Arbitrary eages

Selected poems by
Brenda Read-Brown

For Bettis —
keep writing!
Brenda M. Read-Brown

**For all those people who have encouraged me.
You know who you are.**

ISBN 978-1-291-37690-6

Introduction

Arbitrary edges is a selection of the poems I have written since 1997. Choosing what to include in a collection of work is always difficult; in the end I included the poems I am proud of, the ones I like, and the ones other people like.

I've grouped them, roughly, although of course some poems could have been put in more than one group, but this is, more or less, how they go:

Proper poems, page 4. Some of these have been published in anthologies or magazines.

Performance poems, page 36. These have all been performed for audiences somewhere or other. The idea is that they should be instantly accessible, but leave you with something to think about.

Poems for Pete, page 95. In 1999, I met Pete Brown, a brilliant performance poet. We married on June 2nd 2000, and he died of lung cancer on June 20th 2000. I wouldn't have missed our year together for anything, and the poems, although a bit raw, seem to speak to some people.

Prison poems, page 111. Poems written from my experiences of working with prisoners and young offenders.

Love poems, page 125.

Poems of place, page 156. I write a lot when I'm travelling and on holiday.

Purloined poems, page 176. These poems were inspired by the work of other poets, including Roger McGough, Wilfred Owen, T. S. Eliot, W. H. Auden, Andrew Marvell, Owen Sheers, Henry Reed, John Donne, Elizabeth Barrett Browning... My apologies to them all.

Other poems, page 184. Well, what can I say? They don't all fit into neat categories.

The arbitrariness of edges
It's a bastard to paint,
My cottage. Black and white,
Magpie; timber-framed, chocolate box –
Whatever you call it,
Still a bastard to paint.
No combine harvesters here,
Rolling transformation on the prairie,
But a hand-drawn plough on patchwork fields.
The beams and posts aren't straight, you know –
They meander, pathways stumbled by a drunkard
Seeking a vague lodging.

The first time, you, the painter,
Try to follow lines prescribed by
Predecessors. And you fail.
Later, slowly, comes the clear reality,
In black and white,
That it's up to you to choose.
It's your brush, your paint, your wall,
And every line you take is yours alone,
All edges arbitrary.

Flagship

That summer, when the velodrome in Maida Vale
Focused the sun so cyclists singed,
Every morning, for the season,
I left my nearby lodgings, in short sleeves,
And joined the other scraps of bunting,
Signalling to the bus,
And made my way to Marble Arch,
To Marks and Spencer's flagship store.
Lower than a midshipman,
I was the least important rat,
Selling handbags and silk scarves
Before self-service was the fashion.

I didn't quite salute the suited officers,
Although sometimes I somehow felt I should.
It felt good, in my uniform,
And I understood the rules:
Only married women handled underwear and bedding.
We got eastern princes, buying holdalls
By the dozen – for their concubines, we supposed.
And I made friends with other students,
Like Maria from Finland, who shared my watch,
And teased, but then said *I am only yoking;*
But Linda was permanent, berthed down there for life,
Destined never to be any more than crew.

For me it was all new –
All my meals provided for 20p a day,
As long as I could show
That my nails remained unbitten, my hair neat,
My overall unsmelly, despite the searing heat
That seemed to settle in our basement floor.
Once I was brave in action,
Asked a customer to put out a cigar,
And was promoted: in charge of the umbrellas.
I wheeled them to the door when thunder threatened.

I worked my passage that summer,
For good rations – half-price strawberries and cream –
And I learned that aching feet are the realities of dreams.
But they looked after me; I served them well,
Sailing, retailing under a paternalistic flag.
And when October land was sighted,
I thanked them for the trip,
And resolved that one day I would be
The only captain of my ship.

When ice caps melt
It was funny at first, when a few,
Then many, waddled and cocked their way
Up Oxford Street. But soon, the penguins,
Especially the Emperors, blended with the
Bankers, and apart from complaints about
The odd rockery theft, we stopped paying attention.

It was different, though, when the polar bears
Arrived. We screamed, ran, threw the last lumps of
Rockery; even shot. The streets were bare
Except for restless squats of dirty fur.
But when freezers emptied, markets fell,
We ventured out into life again,

Trying to ignore the grubby thugs on skateboards,
Stolen from now timid youths.
We let them to the front of taxi queues;
Accepted only standing room on buses;
Shrugged at ransacked meat counters.
Some of us made friends; David Attenborough,

Particularly, seemed able to communicate.
Apart from complaints about the odd
Missing person, we stopped paying attention,
Until, on the Embankment first,
Small piles of feathers, black and white, were found.
It started with the penguins.

Bunches

Bunches.
I wore my hair in bunches, beige sprouts
growing from my head,
symmetrical and dangerous,
screwed tight against my scalp
and fastened with elastic,
but waiting to break free and bring me trouble,
because loose hair was against the rules;
set off hair raids at school.
Sometimes, to avoid all this,
I tried a ponytail, but I wanted
to conceal my blushing ears,
and so the bunches stayed for years.

Bunches.
I wanted flowers in bunches
to lay on my father's coffin;
to look as if he'd just walked round the garden,
gathered armfuls of delphiniums and daisies
in a sheaf, with freeform greenery.
I didn't want an *arrangement*, tied with wire,
unnatural, like the hairstyles
I was forced to wear in school.

My mother disapproved,
but I was mistress of my hair by then –
untied, relaxed, unblushing, slightly wild;
and that was how I gave him his last flowers.
In bunches.

Low flying

I don't know exactly what they chat about,
but there is no doubt that geese gossip
as they stocking stitch the sky,
flying in formation.
Listen. Stand out on the lawn.
Let dawn dew tide your slippers dark;
forget the idle doodle of the lark,
and listen. Purposeful as schoolyard mums,
they sideslip, seeking special chums

8

to make arrangements for the day;
discuss the weather, travel plans,
the current leader's lack
of preening skills, which gander
wasn't home last night, the low
demand for quills, how nice
their goslings look, the rising price
of grain. A small skein breaks
away, believing that a cloud's breadth
will give privacy for screaming
secret rumours…
                    and they're gone,
to rake up mud on river banks,
with feet as light as four-by-fours,
and forage for more food for thought
to store up for the evening flight
and pour in baby-waking shrieks
through foul-mouthed, almost human beaks.

Rehearsal

My daughter, learning to walk,
seemed all body and no limbs:
inseparable from sofa cushions,
koala'd round table legs.
Two unsupported steps collapsed her
as a bonfire tumbles
in on itself.
Then one arm is free, a balance pole;
her head appears above the parapet
of fear;
and finally a tiny starfish flies.

On platform 2

On platform 1, boys in a pack
Swing cricket bats at googlies from the future.
A goth complains: he has two D-rings missing –
The legwear he has chosen is high maintenance;
Mud freckles make his leather coat less gloomy,
But his mum says what they need is
A damp sponge.

On platform 2, it seems, a man is dying,
Head lolling like a wind-blown rhododendron.
His wife supports, and with the paramedic,
Drip held shoulder height, looks up from time to time -
Across the line; trains unimportant now,
And ambulances don't run to a timetable.

And what can I do? Nothing.
Shining lengths of high-speed rail
Grow into barbed-wire fences.
My train comes, and a stretcher,
And we set off for our different destinations.

SBB

SBB:
The term that's used by birders
(which is what we have to call them
now that twitching's out of fashion)
for sparrows and the like.
No golden pheasant's boasting;
no magpie's panda clash;
no midnight corvid's brooding,
or flamed kingfisher flash;
just the dull and muddy camouflage
of small brown birds.

What if my angel has no
iridescence in his wings?
I've always, in imagination,
seen him as a swan,
white-hot and frozen,

but suppose he chirps, and doesn't sing?
What if every one of us
has the angel we deserve;
and that cosmic flap I've sometimes heard
comes not from feathered glory,
but a rather larger version of
a small brown bird?

Imaginary
I found myself, the other day,
telling some people I hardly knew
about Roger. Roger Philips.
Rog found me soon after we'd moved house
and, eight years old, I'd gone to a new school.
His father kept horses.
He would take me to see them one day;
teach me to ride bareback;
show me how to fly.

We lost touch later on, when I went to the grammar school
and Roger, now unneeded, was elsewhere.
My mother didn't mention him again,
and I never answered the questions she hadn't asked.

He seemed so real at the time, I said.
It seemed so real as I told them.
I could have done with an imaginary friend
when I was eight, and trying to fit in –
just as the other day, swapping tales with strangers –
but I never had one.

The anarchist manifesto of Henry, one month before his birth
Things will change around here.
All previous patterns of life will become nothing,
As if they had never been.
Those who believed themselves to be powerful
Shall find themselves ruled by another.
The weak will become tyrannical,
And tyrants shall be weak.
All normal communications will cease,
And Babel shall be the king of tongues.
Brick towers will be toppled;
Anything that can be broken, smashed;
Treasures hidden; jewels swallowed;
Books shredded; rubbish revered.
Food shall be thrown, and the frocks
Of evening women vomited upon. Twice.
Mother's milk will be the most desirable sustenance.
Men and women will worship not wealth,
But sleep; there shall be exhaustion
And crying, both the dull and bitter keening
Of fatigue, and the urgent howls of hunger.

But ruling everything will be love,
Looking on tempests but not shaken,
Sacrificing all order for one anarchic soul,
Believing with the zealot's faith
That infancy lasts for just a little while,
And that the rule of law returns
As child grows into youth.
Just as well that they don't know the truth.

The poem I would want to read if I were feeling down...
...would not tell me to pull my socks up,
or myself together.
It wouldn't prattle on about the weather,
or say that worse things happen at sea,
or that there's always someone less well off than me.
It would not tut or roll its eyes;

12

grow impatient; tell me lies;
give me pills;
make me ill.
It would not tell me what to do,
or give me a good talking to.

It would take its time, and smile;
walk with me for a while.
It would hear what I have to say;
perhaps remind me how to play,
and let me find my way.

Hope...
...is delivered with each baby;
is the box round every diamond ring;
it fills the air when children sing.
Begin again! it whispers
to each drunkard who has slipped from grace.
It smiles from every lover's face,
and slouches at each student's side.
It takes you on a fairground ride,
swims by you out to sea;
it's the athlete's personal trainer,
and the artist's promised fee.
It straightens out the collar
of each candidate at interview;
it's born again; it's new
with each bar mitzvah, Eid or christening –
with or without faith, it's always listening.
Hope is everybody's friend;
it gives the high that never ends;
it is the lie that lights the dark
when it lurks in rooms of death,
its truth unsympathetic, stark:
we live, and hope lives with us
   in each dawn
     and every breath.

Talent

She is hungry for young men.
She is the only lonely woman
In the local park on Sundays,
Watching soccer badly played.
She has gladly paid this price of time,
Not for the free kicks of the football fan –
Her goal is different;
She's looking for a man.

Sometimes an older player sees her,
Takes the chance to tease a young full back:
"You could get her in the sack,
"Mate, bet you'd give her one;
"Older women? Gagging for it, son!
"She's dying for a shagging, lad, look,
"You can see the signs!"
It's just a few more lines
In the sad book of men's fun,
But the youngest player blushes,
Says "Fuck off!" and rushes off
To chase a ball, and follow fantasies, and dreams
Of unlaced passions that might rage
With a woman twice his age,
Nearly.
It seems merely a game, to him,
But the deadly flame of just-grown limbs and faces
Draws her to places where he'd play;
A willing prey to need, she hunts him, with a stalker's eye,
Blind to families walking by with dogs,
And the young woman who jogs
Round the pitch, her gaze is fixed
On the bodies of maturing boys;
Ears shut to the haze of sporty noise –
Grunts and thuds and distant whistles –
She just wants to meet her match,
Searching for dark hair and half-shaved bristles,
Hoping that today she'll catch his eye,

And in this injured time they'll know,
Together, the reflection she last saw
In a young child's face, all those years before,
When she had to let him go.

His father played on this park, too,
And she used to watch him then,
So she comes back, again and again,
Scouting not for talent, but for the winning moment when
With a joy no footballer has known,
She can be sure that she has seen
The boy, the son who was her own.
He would be seventeen.

Soulsucker or Never trust a writer
You
find sliced people,
dripping pain.
You hold them tight,
squeeze their stories,
wring out real lives,
told in acid stain;
extract explanations,
draw confessions,
with professions of care
and understanding;
demanding more
until even their skin is bare;
and when
you've scraped away their zest,
taken the pith
all you want,
you consign the rest
to the compost bin,
your creativity fertilised
for worthless words to grow.
You fuck their minds,
and suck their souls,
and then
you let them go.

Lame

Each step conscious, one leg strong,
The other lifted slowly;
The short path to the beach was long
For him, the limping man ahead,
But as I passed he smiled and said
"Pardon; bonjour,"
And his voice reflected the sea's laugh,
And his eyes echoed its unknown turquoise,
And the cormorants he had come to photograph
Shone dark as his hair,
And perched, still, with his poise,
And I felt ashamed
To have thought of him as lame.

And when I returned from sleeping in the sun,
He was sitting, naked, as I passed by;
A sketch drawn with one
Long stroke of ochre; a visible sigh
Of brown skin, thin, carelessly arranged
By an artist's hand upon the rock.
Motionless, he was perfect, nothing could be changed,
And I watched, for minutes, till the clock
Of politeness ticked me off
And struck from me a cough
Of warning. "Bonne journée,"
He said, and smiled
Again, and indeed, beguiled
By the unexpected beauty of the limping man,
Though I found no words to say,
I knew this moment would stay
With me; it was already a good day.

Comfort zone

I live in a nice house
In a nice street
With nice people all around
Whom I never meet,
Except to say hello, how are you;
Perhaps wish happy Christmas;

But we are not listeners.
We greet, and we retreat –
And why should it be different?
We're comfortable; we're ok.

But today,
I went out of my comfort zone
And walked alone
Where wired windows watch from a charity shop;
Where I wouldn't stop,
Not as a rule; not on my own.

And it wasn't nice.
There were rubbish bags,
And filth, and probably rats and mice,
And noise,
And loitering boys,
Who seemed to threaten.
Yet an old black woman smiled
And said good morning.

At least it's clear
What you might be getting into here.
When you go to nice places,
You don't get any warning.

Scars
They fuck you up, your mum and dad,
With all their teasing, twisting, testing.
Thank them. One day you'll be glad –
It's this that makes you interesting.

Undamaged souls, those lucky few,
With parents warm and interactive,
Bore the pants off me and you.
Our scars make us attractive.

Only visiting
It is a home. Not mine –
I'm only visiting
The sick son of a friend.

We perch in the sun and chat,
Interrupted by sedation,
About cricket.
Hesitant wickets break his run of speech.

Another resident is sitting
Sipping plastic lemon squash.

But something is over,
And he rises,
Silent as an anonymous ball boy,
Turns in flight;
Picks up his chair.

He shoulders his burden
And throws.

Howzat!

I am struck,
And out,
Out of the garden
And in through the mad, swinging doors.

This old house
It's just a house I lived in, long ago,
Where sweet smells of tomorrows filled the kitchen
Where I baked dream cakes, hotly vanished
Into future-hungry fingers; and pains and aches
Were banished with the plaster of a kiss,
And Calpol cuddle;
Where childhood sprawled its casual belongings in a muddle,
And the hiss and yowl and spiky fur
Of cats and kids were capped with lids
Of soothing strokes and sorries,

Till the whole place seemed to purr,
And a door was firmly shut on all the worries
Of the office and the world;
And steam curled from companionable coffees
Cashed among a bank of friends,
Whose interest was just care,
And who had always hands to lend
Around a table of shared values,
Or a picnic in the garden,
Where the calling of the curlews
And the slither of the slow-worms
Brought both highs and lows
To living, natural terms.

Not an easy house to live in, though;
Long and thin; communications stretched
Till nerves were twanging; the emotional piano
Badly-tuned, so clanging off-notes jarred the mind,
And real peace was hard to find.
And the plumbing wasn't good.
I used one bathroom, he the other,
So, in two solitary confessionals,
Nasty smells were kept quite private, with locked doors;
When the drains were blocked, we called in the professionals,
Neither of us wanting to face up to sewer truth.
And the bedroom, underneath the unlined roof,
Was always cold.

And now the lies will never be untold,
Or understood; dying, ironically, with him,
In the room designed for living.
The house has been vacated.
The spirits of the place, both good and bad, have been placated.
Now there's nothing there to show
It was once a house where I lived, long ago.

109

Up at the top, on one-hundred-and-nine, the initial sound was muffled;
A baffled thud, a bang; no-one really ruffled;
Even when alarm bells rang,
They sounded silly; shrill;
And, still, when serious loudspeakers sang:
This is no drill, this is no drill,
As they straggled to the exit door,
A gaggle driven from this modern market floor,
Her thoughts were of the bore
Of filing, not in folders, but down
One-hundred-and-nine times eighteen stairs.
Up here, the air still tasted fine;
Her care was all for wasted time, missed deals;
Not life, or just how dying feels.
Fear's knifeblade didn't stroke her spine
Till *Fire!* she heard, passed up the descending line
Of shirts and shoulders, shiny shoes, briefcases and bags;
And still, she hoped this was just rags
Of rumour; a tasteless, humourless joke.
But, seventeen floors down, people came billowing,
Smoke swallowing, following in the opposite direction.

And then, there was no hope;
Not even opportunity for redemption
With an act of selfless sacrifice;
They were cooked and spilt, meaningless grains of rice;
And among so many others, what attention
Would be given to her individual death?

There was no light to read the numbers on the keys;
But she dialled, randomly,
Someone she didn't know, would never see.
And with not quite her final breath,
She left a message on the answerphone:
I just want to say goodbye,
For, in the company of three thousand other souls,
I am about to die, alone.

14th September 2001; suicide bombing of the World Trade Center

Lights, camera, action!
A trilogy

Light work

The village nights are dark and clear –
There are no street lights here;
Burglaries happen in the day,
So we don't need them, anyway;
Houses in the afternoons
In such commuterland communes
Aren't watched by anyone,
Except the lookout.
              No fun,
For night-time runners, though,
Judging where the kerbstones go;
And one solitary path lamp stands,
By a crossing, where, once, holding hands
Was not enough. A child was killed.
Light falls only where blood was spilled.

Cut

It's all in the name of security.
Patient pay-stations hang about at the edges
Of the small-hours small-town car park,
Ledges mottled in the dark
With human droppings, of no-longer gooey chewie,
Ash and fag-ends, shopping's precursor.
"Charges apply on Sundays and bank holidays"
Fusses the sign.
But a malign and terser
Message comes from their big-brother structures.
Summer-night silence ruptured
Here, by whirring, not from night-jar's wings,
Or sleepy noises from generator,
Pregnant with generous energy.
The late-night returning driver
Asks himself what sings
Above, from time to time,
With distant menace, unalive, a
Death rattle.

It is the night-watchman's noisy mime;
CCTV; the residents' friend,
An electric fence for unruly young cattle,
Changing its stance to take in a varying view;
Indifferent to differences: floodlit pools,
Lakes of darkness, temperature or seasons –
To the panoramic camera they're all the same.
It doesn't know the reasons
For its hide-and-seek game.
It doesn't stop to admire strings of dew jewels
Hanging from a tree,
Or look longingly at the legs
Of a raucous passing hen-party.
It doesn't stop to have a cup of tea.
It's all in the name of security.

And on the thousandth revolution
Of its nocturnal tireless traffic,
Will its picture's resolution
Capture the still eloquence, the graphic
Image of a single yellow butterfly,
Pinned against a dark car,
With a star's purity?

Man's ingenuity has come far,
In the name of security.

Performance
Uniformed and uniform,
Peak-capped and polyester-quilted,
Two guards at the gate make stilted
Conversation as they check credentials.
Then no-one comes for a while.
But an idler watches with a smile,
An unseen agent, confidential,
Outside for a cigarette break,
As in formation, the pair pace
Either side of a wall, come face-to-face
With mock-dramatic double take;
Each raise one arm and leg, half

A mirror image; do it again, and laugh,
Then penguin-waddle, flapping arms.
Giggle-seized they dance and hug.

The distant audience, charmed,
Can't help but clap.
And with a shy, embarrassed shrug,
Accepting that they have been trapped
In performance, they both bow.
They're human, anyhow.

****

Routine measure

It's just a tiny shadow on a screen.
Perhaps it's just where tissues overlap.
No bigger than a pea, although not green,
But still, it's made me think – dying is crap.

I'm sure that I can feel it, on the right.
I know that they're good odds – nineteen to one;
Don't know if it's sixth sense or second sight –
I'm sure this is a bet I haven't won.

It's just a routine measure, so they say;
Some extra X-ray pictures; ultrasound;
A physical exam to rule out doubt.
They'll tell me the prognosis the same day,
That is, if they know what it is they've found.
But I just want to rip the bugger out.

Solitary

Sickness admits of no sharing.
Even sympathy, assistance, caring
Are for the fortunate only;
And pain is lonely.

No-one can take the burden –
Illness is like sin;
No visitor can get inside
The prison of our skin;
And the mental walls are thicker
As the chances grow more thin.

There is no company
In a hand held when we die.
Of course I will be with you
Is a well-meant, shallow lie –
We sidle through the narrow gate,
It's a single-file goodbye,
And the questions differ: going,
We ask *what?*; and staying, *why?*

Pruning

You choose the right shoot, and you cut it;
A different method for each type of tree;
Some strengthened by struggling for sunshine,
Some needing space to be free;

And you shout at the branch you're attacking,
"I just have to do this, okay?"
But the steel of the blade is still lacking
From your heart, which wants its own way.

But red pencils and pruners create things –
All the flowery phrases must go;
Too much growth interferes with the bees' wings;
Crowded words don't allow thought to show.

So this is creative destruction,
A selfish sacrifice to the good,
And without this positive reduction,
Poems are no more than dead wood.

I'm suffering from stress

I'm suffering from stress.
I have to handle kids all day -
You wouldn't believe the things they say!
And from nine, when I join in the fray,
There's six whole hours till I get away,
And without thirteen weeks' holiday,
I'd never cope; I couldn't stay
With the difficulties of teaching; yes,
I'm suffering from stress.

I'm suffering from stress.
On Mondays I get on a plane;
Wednesdays, usually a train;
My P.A. will sort out my chain
Of transport; I hate all the pain
Of travelling – Paris, Rome, Bahrain –
A meeting, food, then back again,
No sleep to rest my wearied brain;
It's all first class, of course, the strain
Of sitting near the noise and mess
Would be too much – I'm suffering from stress.

I'm suffering from stress.
I lost my job two months ago,
But so far my family doesn't know;
I leave the house, nowhere to go,
Each morning; hope it doesn't show
I'm telling lies. Cash is running low –
I can't bear this; the kids will be so
Upset when they find that this year there's no
Holiday; worse, that at one blow,
Everything has gone, and dad is less
Than a man, now; yes,
I'm suffering from stress.

I'm not suffering from stress,
Merely hunger. I have no food to eat.
I must walk miles to get a drink.
My children have all gone to meet
Their maker, whoever that is. To think
Or worry takes more energy and care
Than I have left. All you out there,
May your God continue to bless
You with all good things. Yes,
I'm luckier than you – I have less;
I have no need to gamble or guess
About tomorrow. I'm not suffering from stress.

Honey summers
They were honey summers, then;
Slow-motion golden drops
Between spring's spoon and autumn's crust;
No thunderstorms of future, just
The buttercups of June.
This sort of season never stops,
For memory again
Renews the dewdrops on the spiders' webs
With a tide that flows but never ebbs;
Makes you lie on grass as soft as silk,
Scattered with spills of daisy milk;
Brings back the hushed and still warm dusks
Of rose and honeysuckle musk.

And so it never goes away,
Though you're here in life's November;
It only takes the odd warm day
And you're there; and you remember.

Written white

Happiness writes white, a poet said.
This morning, happiness is everywhere;
Scribbled, splashed on gardens, hills and streets –
An unexpected gift from shivering angels.
And grown-ups all remember how to play.
Beneath the ski-suits, mufflers and hats,
In Technicolor, everybody smiles.

Universal metaphysics

It is a paradox, quite metaphysical;
I think it concerns relativity.
My requirements are simple, but then again quizzical –
Independence but yet reactivity.

I want to share time; the space is all yours,
But somehow it's equally mine;
Planets whose paths run a parallel course,
On a touching elliptical line.

To put it in words that are terse:
I want you, not your universe.

Seagulls

They call this work. So, what have I done today?
I have watched a shoal of fishes save my screen;
I have made two cups of coffee, and three teas, and been
To the loo at least four times;
I spent an hour trying to find good rhymes
For "Aegean", but, sadly, failed;
I have studied the yacht on the calendar as it sailed,
Bright and wild, across the azure Aegean,
And passed half an hour thinking of me an'
You lying in the sun together;
I discussed the outlook for tomorrow's weather
With the gateman, and my boss, and the stationery girl,
Who never leaves her cupboard;
I doodled through two meetings, and then rubbered
Out my little sketches, in case they were seen,
And analyzed for hidden meanings,
Or taken as evidence of my leanings
Towards indolence,
A sign that I'm not as keen
As I profess to be.

I stared through my window at all I could see –
The blinded glass of the office blankly facing,
And the grey clouds chasing –
Without terms of reference,
No need for defiance or deference –
Across a box of sky;
And the seagulls, whose job it is to fly,
And whose working world consists of being free.
I suppose that here inside it's warm and dry,
And I won't be struck by occupational injury –
Except, as all computer users do,
Terminal boredom; but perhaps the crew
On the yacht, and even the seagulls, get sick of the sea.
But what makes me most concerned
Is the lesson I have learned
Today; that the person sitting in my chair isn't really me.

Poem or list?

I was married to a poet –
Not for long, for now he's dead.
But whenever I sat up in bed,
Switched on my bedside light to write,
He always roused himself and said,
"Hey babe, poem or list?"
Are you Brahms or are you Liszt,
Are you drunk with words or just pissed
Off with life?
'Cos drinking alcohol is optional,
It's what we want to do,
But life's processes can't be delayed –
Eventually, we have to find a loo.

And that's what writing lists is –
Making fences round abysses,
Sealing knots and sticking labels;
It's like learning your times tables –
A planned escape from fables,
Myths, and all that fuzzy stuff,
Cause we try but never get enough control
Of things that have no soul.

So who says that escapism is
In poetry and stories?
Making lists may seem a bore
But it's a way you can pretend
That the drudgery has an end
Before you die;
But in poems we accept
That whatever their effect –
If you laughed or if you wept –
Every word of every poem is a lie.

See any Post House foyer, at coffee time
Shirts and ties and talking heads;
Silver pens in laundered hands;
Other people's money sheds
Its shine in businessland,
So buffed-up words slip easy
From the tongues of polished men;
Truth's friction cannot hold the sleazy
Fiction that they spend;
Polygraphs a rising trend,
With all the other charts displayed,
Projected profit prophecies the end
Game duplicitously played.

Guarded eyes hide double bluffs;
Trump cards concealed in double cuffs;
The pretty wrapping's not enough
To keep the stench held in;
Slimy smiles beckon and cajole,
Thin covers over stinking holes;
These suits hold sewage in place of souls,
Wrapped in a one-way skin.

How sweet would be this smooth seduction,
An effortless, slippery introduction,
A vortex with such burnished suction –
Relax, and you'll be drawn in;
But their shiny shoes reflect your face,
Look hard! If you don't see any trace
Of conscience, then stay in this place
With them, and you'll fit in;

Or if you think your values better than this world of gilded tin,
Think twice – there is no doubt: we all have our personal sin.

Working for a living

I could have penned a pretty poem today,
Or spoken a soft sonnet;
Found a theme from nature,
Written variations on it;
Expressed the milk and honey of thoughts flowing round my head –
But I went into work instead.

I could have swum the channel of our sheets,
And stroked your back at length;
Crawled into your comfort
When your breaststroke sapped my strength,
And skinny-dipped quite shameless in the warm depths of our bed –
But I went into work instead.

I could have climbed high on a hill,
And tasted sweet rain falling;
Seen a shadow slipping,
Been haunted by hawks calling;
Looked for the path less trodden, and followed where it led –
But I went into work instead.

And you never hear of the dying,
Between forgetting and forgiving,
Wasting their last breath in sighing
Final words that should never be said:
"I wish I'd spent less time on living,
"And gone into work more instead."

Cat bite

The cat bites; a fierce cat
On sly mornings.
I walk downstairs; it bites,
It scratches. I have warnings;
I see it, waiting, for pleasure
With furry pain, which I don't avoid.

Cats have dirty mouths.
They wash, oh, they wash;
They want to be thought clean;
But their teeth
Hold venom, their mouths
Are full of filth and lies.

And this time, the puncture
Was deep. I didn't bother
With sticking plaster. No repair
Kit for cat's bared grin,
Hypodermic teeth through skin.
I have thin ankles,

But this one grows thicker now.
It swells; it slows me,
Ties me down. Fight, white cells,
Against black cat's unluck;
It will do no good.
This cat knows me.

It knows how to hurt,
When it strokes others.
There are many cat lovers,
Including me.
It presents me with dead feathers,
Mouse entrails, paws,

But this insidious gift lives,
Lives on me, in me;
Makes me stiff, awkward.
I am no longer upright.
I am throbbing red, dead body white.
I no longer see things clearly.

I could seek help,
But for what? Once bitten,
Twice lied to, I hide
The signs of advancing poison.
I am ashamed
Of wanting this.

It will reach my heart;
I hope; there will be numbness.
The cat jumps on my bed,
Asking, still, to be fed.
And it washes. We conspire
To keep secret the cause of death.

Sleeplessness
We are given sleep
As a dark hole to crawl into,
A black door
To close on the crucifixions of consciousness,

And wakefulness to keep
Us aware of the omnipotence
Of angels; a floor
To stand on and face night's namelessness;

For we have the need to weep
With the gods, who know all,
And yet to know no more
Than animals do of life's pointlessness.

Dolphins

I could have swum with dolphins.
I could have traced a wandering path
To dreamscape places where the faces
Smile with the sun,
And aren't familiar as your embrace is
To me now.
I could have climbed through fine-drawn pines,
Reached peaks that pierce the sky,
And looked down to where the sea-birds fly
Over waves that perform, and bow, and die,
And disappear in the ocean where
I could have swum with dolphins.

I could have danced with princes.
I could have nightwatched owls, and purred with pussycats,
And dined where quince is
Favourite food;
But I turned my back and said goodbye
To the music that seduces,
And the dreams poetry induces,
The persuasive sun's insistence,
The persistence of the mountains
And the dolphins' curdling cry,
When I looked at you and said *I
Will.*

With the smooth skill of a charmer
You disarmed me, tamed me, tied me;
Swooned me and cocooned me
In an armour of defences.
No expenses spared, you paid my bills
And my price,
Surrounded me with niceness,
Coated me in cashmere and candy floss.
The distant sense that I had lost
Things far away grew farther away,
And if I saw a shooting star, the
Wish I made was for life to be – okay.

But now the lover's blanket I am wrapped in
Grows threadbare; seams snapped;
I am worn rough with irritation,
And where there was a feather bed, there
Now is suffocation;
I am trapped,
And must escape.

But the teeth of your smile are tipped with aggression,
And keeping me here is an obsession –
My departure would be like rape
For you.
This is not love; it is possession,
An expression of control.
I am held fast, and must forget
That there was a time when yet
I could have drunk the sun,
And brightened at a star's spark;
But my fickle will won't learn its part,
And the supple, subtle murmurings still tickle
My ears, and my heart;

But there is nothing to be done.
Awareness is a hard kiss,
And because, although, I am swallowed by the darkness
Of my fears,
I must know the truth, however stark –
I could have swum with dolphins,
But I rejected this,
And chose to be protected, owned and guarded
By a shark.

Cross-expressing

I am a serious woman, with a wardrobe full of suits
And elegant high-class dresses – no room for thigh-high boots.
I think gender is a gift from God, and I keep my body pure,
But a curious compulsion lurks behind my closet door.
I try to keep it under wraps, but my poems let me down.

We should treat art with reverence, with a careful, thoughtful frown,
And Ted Hughes and Sylvia Plath are poets I really strive to follow,
But in my writers' circle, the applause sometimes seems hollow,
'Cause when they clap, it's so polite – restrained, reflective ripples,
While here we can cheer odes on chocolate, laugh at lines about
        willies and nipples!

My boyfriend is a poet too; T.S.Eliot's his hero,
But, rearranged, he's just toilets (think about it), and
        his giggle content's zero;
So, like a man who puts on his wife's clothes when he's out of her sight,
I have a hidden hobby – yes, I am a transversite.
I swap designer-label imagery for performer's doublet and hose;
The haiku's perfect symmetry for rhymed couplets and red nose!
And – oh, thanks for letting me confess; I know it isn't nice,
But it's great to be with guys who might understand this secret vice.
Though they say it's iniquity, they tell me it's no good,
Among ubiquitous obliquity, I long to be understood,
And yes, I can write sonnets – metaphors dancing down the page –
But I'd rather entertain or energise; enthral, enrage, engage;
And I really like just dressing up and standing on a stage!

But, though he's a left-wing liberal, this my boyfriend can't accept,
Though I'm supposed to tolerate the secrets that he's kept,
So we've come to an arrangement: just once a month we're free;
He does what he wants to do; I can be the real me.
So here I am to let rhyme rip, with poetry that rocks;
Cross-expressing with my partner, who stays home,
        dressed in my frocks.

Mind the gap

His eyes were deep brown –
Not pools, exactly, because let's face it,
Pools are usually full of algae and weed
And other things you really don't need
Like scum, and giant pike that would delight
In taking a bite out of your thumb,
Or more important parts;
And his eyes weren't like that.
No. They shot chocolate darts;
Not Cadbury's or Galaxy,
More the dark organic fairtrade kind,
The sort you only find
In health food shops or Oxfam,
Or a really posh branch of Tesco.
Somehow I knew that he was vegan.
We met al fresco,
And my knees began to weaken
As the sun reflected from his head,
Which had been shaved –
Not in an aggressive, footballerish kind of way,
Not at all like David Beckham;
Probably, I reckoned, to hide
Incipient male-pattern baldness;
But it seemed engraved
With just-grown stubble,
Begging to be stroked,
And I knew I was in trouble.
This was my kind of bloke.

He was wearing shorts.
Not those awful long shorts,
That always turn my thoughts to boys
Wearing trousers they've outgrown.
No. They were above his knees,
So his legs were fully shown – poised,
Walker's legs, strong as trees –
Though not old and gnarled like oaks,
Or willowy like …willows;
More like elms (without the disease)
Or – yes, beech.

We went to the beach
At 2 am,
And swam naked, under a full moon,
And made love in the still-warm surf,
And I thought to myself,
How badly named that washing powder was,
Though to say Ariel or Persil wouldn't have seemed right;
Not even Tide,
Because this was the Mediterranean.

I tried to hide
My flabby thighs and wrinkled face,
Because on that night and in that place
It was as good as it could possibly be.
But now, the problems I can clearly see:
He is fifteen years younger than me
And he lives in Sheffield.
I kept my disappointment concealed –
Not because of Sheffield,
Though that was bad enough,
But because of all the stuff
People would say –
Cradle-snatching; toyboy;
Young enough to be her son.

Our relationship has begun,
But it's reached an awkward stage
Because he does not yet know my age.
And I must face this unwitting deception,
Because it's not a minor discrepancy,
And it's not in the right direction.
Whatever my perception
Of our bold and surfy orgasm – oh gosh! -
It will, one day, all come out in the wash,
And it is a chasm, I mean – a ravine:
My age minus his is **fifteen!**
But – *I* don't mind the gap,
And double standards are crap,
So for now I'll stick to my cunning plan.
And keep my age hidden as long as I can
Under wrinkle remover and fake instant tan;

Only fools measure age merely by elapsed years,
And this lie's justified, though some people might sneer,
But everyone knows that the whole world would cheer
If he were a woman and I …
         were a man.

Cox

Cox.
I love them.
I love to take them in my mouth,
Put their firmness to the test.
I think that English Cox are best,
But I'm open to Cox from any nation.
I hate those times of Cox starvation,
When I'm obliged to go without,
Make do with lesser pleasures.
In my hunger I remember
The sweet hardness of my smooth-skinned treasures,
And look longingly to September's end,
When harvest time begins again,
And once more my teeth are nipping
At a Cox's Orange Pippin.

George Clooney

Let's face it, you're not George Clooney.
And you won't dance.
And you snore.
And you're a bit on the poor side.
And you have a passion for elevator music.
And you never tell me that you love me.

Still, you might not have George Clooney's looks,
But can he cook?
When I say I'm in a hurry and I've only time for toast,
You just rustle up Thai curry with a host
Of fragrant flavours; you're the saviour of my taste buds;
Make them blush and go all silly
With that sweet and frilly – thing – made of meringue
And sunshine mango. And though you'll never dance,
You put my tummy in a trance.
And my tongue performs a tango
When you say *Here's lentil stew.*
I made it just for you because I know you don't like meat,
And you sit and watch me eat.
And once I said I wished that you would tell me how you feel,
And you said *I don't do words,*
But I'm telling you I love you every time I cook a meal.

Now, the elevator music – that's much harder to forgive –
I mean, why? Really, why?
But you give me your time and your skill at diy –
You're as handy with a spanner as a wok.
You've made my house and garage rock.
Underneath your watchful eye,
All my devices run like clockwork,
And my pushbike has been tuned until it sings.
You've put the rhythm in my swing seat;
Out of discord you've made harmony;
From chaos you've brought calm for me;
You've polished up my car for me,
And never missed a beat –
With technician's syncopation;
And my electrics are no longer in breach of regulations
Concerning safety and health,

And I'm not in any doubt
That you're telling me you love me when you get your hammer out.
And when we do that thing in bed,
You really hit the nail right on the head.

So, I must ignore the snoring, though it's loud and deeply boring
And I'm really short of sleep; I'm almost weeping with fatigue,
And it's not from too much bonking – rather that your nasal honking's
In a steeply different league from other men.
But when I bruise you in the kidneys once again to stop the din,
You sometimes turn to face me, murmur *Sorry* and embrace me,
And the susurrus of your breathing weaves new dreams for my delight;
You're telling me you love me when you hold me in the night.

I guess you're ok as you are.
And how could I forget that the first time that we met,
You took me to a film in which George Clooney was the star?
In fact, your niceness never stops.
You like to help me shop,
Even though you are not gay –
That's something not found every day; in my experience it's rare
To find a man who really cares about accessories.
And, what's even better is – you make me laugh – you're funny!
George Clooney may have money, and he has my casual lust,
But honey, you're the one I'd trust,
Not just for company and fun, but to choose
          my new shoes and matching handbag,
And that's something you can brag about, although of course
          you wouldn't;
You couldn't, any more than you could whisper *I love you*,
Or break your mind-numbing cds (oh please! oh please!) in two;
But you show me that you love me with everything you do.
So I've said no to George Clooney; I want you.

Assault

It's always, always the same,
And you've only got yourself to blame –
But you're feeling fit, and all lit up,
In your tent, and kitting up:
Boots, backpack, rollups, ready rolled,
Cold water to avoid dehydration
Tablets, lighter – enough preparation,
And it's over the top and into the noise.
The pop-pop-pop of unadjusted mikes;
The squeak of person-powered generator bikes;
The werewolf howl of an untuned voice;
The tsunami growl of untamed guitars;
The wandering cries of unwanted kids,
All painted up as tigers and lost as stars,
And it's all so bloody loud.
You can't see the main stage because of the crowd,
And the mud is like something out of the trenches,
And in the loos, the stench is
Of death, from chickpea curry.
So you hold your breath and hurry back
To the second stage,
Where a singer who is falling off the page of fame
Falls off the edge of the platform and flattens a nearly naked girl,
And batons twirl and there's almost a riot;
And you're searching for somewhere for a quiet smoke;
Perhaps a tiny toke. Or two.
A woman in white drifts by you, ten feet high.
She is on stilts. Why?
And munchies strike.
No! You're not taking your turn on the person-powered generator bike –
You went without lunch and you need a bacon sandwich.
But the bacon baps have all been sold;
The last ostrich burger is burnt and cold
And there's nothing but alfalfa sprouts and bleeding falafels.
The smell of incense is making you ill,
You just can't cope;
All hope is gone.
And you might as well take that suicide pill… but wait!
What's that they're playing?
You *love* that song!

You strain to hear your favourite lines,
And your memories have tears, and they taste of sad wine;
You wave your lighter though no-one can see;
You've even forgotten you needed a pee,
And you lie down on wet grass, and sing, sing along,
And dream and doze…

And wake, to find your money's all gone,
As it always goes,
Sucked up by this carnival of harmony and laughter.
It is the morning after,
And you blag some cash,
And buy a bleeding falafel in a bun,
You're not surprised that it tastes like dung.
You didn't sign up for this,
And your battle against nature has not been won –
Your bladder is begging you for a piss.
So you take a pee behind a tree,
And retreat to your camp,
Get out of your damp clothes
And into your even damper sleeping bag,
And close your eyes,
But you can't shut out the distant whine of Billy Bragg,
And you realise that once again you haven't even copped a shag.

It's always, always the same,
And you've only got yourself to blame,
And it's a mystery
That, like politicians, you do not learn from history,
But every time forget the war you went through the year before, when
You swore you'd never, ever, ever go to a festival
Again.

V for vanilla

It's always, always the same,
And I've only got myself to blame.
But it's in my blood - I did Greenham Common,
And things like that aren't soon forgotten.
In my day, we knew how to be naughty -
Not like these kids today, just drunk on WKD40,
Or whatever they call it.

Anyway, in my bag I carry a flag -
Not with revolution's burning flame
In red and black; no, a Zimmer frame,
In cream and latte, with pensioner rampant!
I founded this new old-age party;
Stripped off my camouflage and khaki;
Smart casual, now, and a zip-up cardi.

It was time for us to demonstrate,
No shouting; we'd just remonstrate.
We weren't looking for vendetta.
We were after something better,
And our slogan is a killer -
V for vanilla!

We had postcards - not placards; the others wouldn't risk it -
That said important things like: *No VAT on biscuits!*
Down with things that we don't like!
Support the Daily Mail! I banned that one.
More Emmerdale at the weekends!
A whiter shade of pale!

Anyway, as I said to the arresting officer,
We never meant to start a rumble,
With that drive-by in our hood.
We wound the windows down to grumble,
And you know, we grumble good.

And we weren't fuelled by Jack - just Tesco value Sauvignon,
And when that chap said W*hat's yo beef, man?* and I answered:
      Bourguignonne,
I didn't intend any disrespect, but it all kicked off with that,
And a walking stick's quite handy when they've knocked off
      your best hat,
And I know I should have wisdom; should be granny who knows best
But I couldn't resist yelling *Fucking pigs!* and I had to resist arrest,

We set out to protest mildly at what annoys us all,
Like low-slung jeans that show boys' pants; print that's far too small;
Long waiting lists for hip ops; cyclists without lights;
The groups of large young people who frighten us at night.
But we wouldn't speak out loudly or the hooligans might hear,
And they know we're growng older, and they know we feel the fear
Of loss - not just our gloves and specs,
But youth, power, love, respect;
wealth, influence, health, mobility,
safety, security, dignity, stability,
autonomy, authority, worth, personality,
confidence, independence, driving licences, senses, sense,
our homes, our rights, our friends;
in fact everything that makes life worth living,
and finally life itself.

But no-one loves you when you moan; no-one wants to hear us rage,
And puce doesn't go with older skins, we should hide ourselves
      in beige.
But I didn't, and I'm here in the cells again. It's always, always
      the same,
And if that loo in the corner stinks, I've only myself to blame -
Prison food's worse than bleeding falafels - I was on the bog all night,
And it's here in this cell where I sleep and eat - some things
      just aren't right.
But my cellmate's lent me a book to read; I'll start on it today.
It's clearly meant for us, 'cause it's called *Fifty shades of grey,*
And I hope it'll give us new ideas on how we can get our way
Because at last I've learned from history. This is the moment when
I swear I'll never, ever, ever demonstrate again.

Fiery Jack

The pain seems to be muscular; each night a new attack,
Sometimes in his chest, but more often in his back.
At last he's found something to ease
The pangs; you take the tube and squeeze
And apply the Fiery Jack.

He rubs some round his nipple;
I massage it the length of his spine,
And when I hear the soft breath of his relief
I feel a mounting, excited belief
That now, this time, this time
We will make love at last,
Because the pain for now has passed
To the dark parts of his mind;
But this peace of body will be brief –
I know we must move fast;

For though the pleasure of his company
Is a never-ending thrill for me
I need this space of pain-free leisure
To enjoy the company of his pleasure.

And so the loving starts;
A collection of caresses,
A confection of sweet somethings,
The joint joy which more or less is
How it always goes with us;

The easy choreography of a couple tuned
And touching,
Tongue to lip, chest to breast, fingertip to inner thigh,
And higher, till, with synchronized sigh,
Stand-in hands rehearse what is to come;
And oh! His fingers and his thumb,
And Oh!! An unexpected sting –
A fingernail perhaps? – you know the sort of thing –
But not enough to stop the need, the yearning,
And at last he is inside me, we're relearning
The sweet rhythm, and he turns to me and says
Brenda, d'you feel burning?

And then, oh Christ, it hurts!
Drowsy senses shocked alert
By sharp sand with chilli powder mixed
To a searing paste and spread betwixt
Our legs – or so it seems.
We fall apart, transfixed,
Thoughts race, raging, to dangerous places –
Allergy? Disease?
Incompatibility? Unease
Crumples both our faces,
But then at once light gleams –
Is it the lingering of our fingering
With the muscle embrocation?
Unwittingly, for lubrication
We've used not natural juices, saliva or KY –
The memory all comes back:
We've spread the ointment in the fly,
And fucked with Fiery Jack.

Gods
In the beginning, omniscient as I am,
I knew that soup would one day would be a starter,
So that's where I began –
With soup, primeval, a gloop; something like gravy,
Though not savoury or sweet.
Neat! I thought, but too much like what would one day
Be school dinners. Time to begin again.
My first creature – well, to be honest, it didn't come out that well;
A single cell. It didn't even squeal when I gave it a prod.
I thought *Oh, God!* – well, actually, *Oh, me!*
Creature number two was an aquatic worm, a spineless eel,
All it could do was turn,
So I moved straight on to number three – a fish –
But I still hadn't got the hang.
Not having any fins it never swam,
And with no gills it couldn't breathe; looked sickly;
It died quite quickly.
Creature four was swift and sure,
But had no eyes; kept bashing into rocks,
And, despite its size, was soon snapped up by number five,

Which had fins, gills, vision and teeth – all it needed to survive,
Until it met number six – the shark;
But even that didn't like the dark,
And I'd made night and day aeons before; much too late to change.
Creature seven was kinda strange – it kept flinging itself up on the sand.
It seemed to want to be on land –
But already, I was dissatisfied;
It seemed no matter what I tried, my creatures weren't on side –
They didn't tell me jokes, sing psalms;
Entertain with witty repartee.
And I knew I'd have to make billions more
Before they even thought about TV.
And they had no faith, or doubt;
There was definitely something I'd left out.

Anyway, back to creature number eight,
Which met its fate with number six, the shark,
As did nine, ten, eleven, twelve and indeed
Thirteen to twenty. The shark had seed, in plenty,
And sowed it; it had learned to breed.
So I went large – yes, we have fast food in heaven -
And bulked up creature number seven.
Two flavours: one with fearsome teeth and armour;
The other huge, but wouldn't harm a fly.
They fought; they died.
Ages went by, literally,
And meanwhile I pondered bitterly about what I had done –
Still my creatures weren't much fun,
And I couldn't think of a solution, so I invented evolution
And left them to it.
Oh, I called in from time to time.
Forty-one million and ninety-nine
Engendered quite a fuss; it looked very much like us,
Only crouched and covered over with hair,
But I had stuff to do elsewhere;
Plenty of planets to play with out there.
And it was only recently that I popped in again,
To find that now they call themselves men,
Though really they are little boys
Who treat like toys the cells that I have given them.
But

They write poems and make laws; they love; they hate;
They're cruel and kind; shine smiles, shed tears;
They try and fail; they think; create;
They are genetic engineers.
I wanted creatures just like me,
And now, at last, after all these years,
That's what they've turned out to be –
Against almighty odds,
They are not worms or sharks:
I have made gods.

Happy Hoover

When you're snorting through a twenty
And you think that you've got plenty,
Well, you know you always lose a little bit;
And show me the pot smoker
Who, preparing his next toke or
Two, doesn't drop some little crumbs of shit;
And if you're depressed and ill
Fumbling for your Prozac pill,
Hell, it slips! and it gets kicked under the door;
Well, all these dandy dregs of drugs
Stay on carpets, boards and rugs
And make me happy! Cause, you know, this is *my* floor.
And though really she's a slut,
Sometimes my owner gets off her butt,
And takes me out to roam around the room;
And among the dust and fluff
Is all this wild and wacky stuff,
That makes my little motor go vroom! Vroom!

So I'm a happy Hoover.
I'm a groovy kind of mover,
And I do my work with lots of silly smiles;
I coast on coke and drone on dope
Spend cupboard days cooped up in hope
Of evenings grazing over mats and tiles.
But I can never roll my own,
I pick up pebbles but don't get stoned,
And mushroom trimmings just can't make me high;

So each time you take a trip,
Please be sure to leave a tip,
And my happy Hoover head will hit the sky!

Or you'll see a meaner cleaner,
Less a Dyson, more Mike Tyson,
And then the fur will really start to fly,
'Cause if I don't get my sweeties,
I'll suck off your fucking feeties,
So be messy! Or you'll make your Hoover cry.

But I know that it's no good
And I really think you should
Be much more careful what you scatter on the lino,
For like every junkie and wino
I'd really like to quit this scene;
In fact, this Hoover just wants to be clean.

But hey, man, that's a drag!
So help me skin up in my bag;
Drop me the odd E,
Or a tab of LSD;
Fill your place with spacedust,
Wipe the frown from off my face, just
Keep on mixing it with all your dirt and muck,
And remember, if your life's a vacuum – well, mine sucks.

Frog princess

She was a bit of a slag, if you know what I mean –
Sat there on the pavement where the dog shit had been.
In fact, let's be honest, she was ugly as sin –
I've seen prettier muck in the depths of my bin.
And thin as a Twiglet, but without all the bumps,
And as for her clothes – for Christ's sake, what a frump!
They were saggy and baggy, and all frayed and grey,
And I'd've walked straight past on an ordinary day,
But this time I leaned over and flipped her a quid.
I'll admit it - that's the kind of thing that I did
To impress the girls – I'd come over all caring;
They'd go *Oh, how sweet!* and pretend that they shared in
My sympathy, then – simples! –I'd got them in bed.
But the girl with me this time, she just scowled, and said,
Why the fuck you give money to that little tart?
And I thought, *Hang on, Angie – have a heart!*
She might look like litter, like anyone's whore,
But – there but for the grace of; her life could be yours.
You're no different to her, really, under the skin.
You might act prim and proper, but I know you'll give in.
'Cause I was a looker, see; yeah, I was fit.
I could turn on the charm, splash the smile round a bit.
I'd love them and leave them. Well, I never got hurt –
Why waste any feelings on some bit of skirt?
So I said, *You don't own me. I'll have who I like.*
Got a problem with that? Well, get on your bike.
She said *Who d'you think you are? Taking the piss!*
Well, I dare you – you want her, just give her a kiss!
This was going too far – I deserved more respect,
So took on the dare – not what she'd expect.
I looked down at the pavement girl – God, what a skank;
The last picture you'd choose to help you with a – anyway,
It weren't gonna be easy. I screwed my eyes shut,
Deep breaths, so I wouldn't get a whiff of the slut;
Closed my mind – I'd never been near such a dog;
Then I went for it; gave her a proper good snog.
And everything shimmered, like a silvery fog,
And she said *Merci.* She'd turned into a frog!
Well, a woman, but French, like; dressed in haute couture,
And gorgeous; she smiled and said *Merci, monsieur!*

And I fell in love. I dumped Ang there and then;
I embraced my grenouille, and I kissed her again.
And I knew all the lingo - Jacques le garçon no more
My life changed for ever; I was suddenly sure.
Oh, I'd been a bad boy – though I did have some fun –
But everything was different now I'd found the one.

This mam'selle had me captivé; I could see our futures blending,
So like any fairy tale this story has a happy ending.
And Angie? She's been helping with the homeless ever since,
But she'll have to kiss a lot of frogs before she finds her prince.

Slam dunk
Yo! I'm nearly forty-nine, and I've tried to fill my time;
I've smoked some funny cigarettes and drunk a lot of wine;
I've travelled the free and the unfree world;
I've had my share of lovers – always men, never a girl.
It's not that I'm prejudiced – my oldest friend is gay;
It's just the inclination never came my way.
But that's an aside; so anyway -

I've been a performer, though I never went to RADA;
Sometimes I've had lots to eat, sometimes an empty larder;
I've walked down the Grand Canyon, and back up, which is
        much harder,
Driven Minis, Lamborghinis – but not, thank God, a Lada.

I can cook, do maths and sew, I can play the piano
(Pia, pia, piano, piano, pia..)
I've been on the radio, and a television show
(Just a quiz – a good one though).
I've climbed Kilimanjaro,
I've dived and skied and skated;
I'd have finished … the marathon … if only …they'd waited.

I've been a mother twice, and three times I've been a wife,
And so good, so far it's been a pretty full life.
And sometimes people ask me if there's nothing I can't do,
Well, of all the things I've tried, I have failed always in two,
And in these I just can't succeed at all:

They're relationships (aaah) and *basketball.*
They both have me stumped, however high or much I've jumped,
And I couldn't score a basket – I'll never be that tall,
However much I practise bouncing up and down my hall,
But my boyfriend's an American I met last fall!
I can't play the game he loves, but I love the games he plays,
And I want to make it last this time; I tried to think of ways
I could keep his interest growing (without the effort showing)
And knowing he liked poems of a very special kind, I set my mind,
Though I thought it was boring crap – went on and on without a gap –
Please feel free to take a nap – to write rap.

So I would speak in an American accent
With pauses in odd places, to say that I've been sent
On a mission I was given
To that free and unfree world
To tell each man and every woman, every boy and every girl
That they can sit in their homes and write cool pomes
With no obsession with aggression, oppression, dispossession;
The suggestion that creation is related to frustration and by implication –
       basketball,
And I'll say this all
Time after time after time after time after (and do you know, I really
began to enjoy all this stuff!)
time after time
And I won't be satisfied
Until the happiness that makes the whole world rhyme
Is mine!
And I will succeed where in the past I have not,
In love *and* basketball I'll give it one more shot,
'Cause I don't give up, never, and this love could last for ever –
Though however much he asks, I can't put on two feet in height,
Push that ball down through the basket; but I might win a slam one night
('Cos now I *don't* think rap is junk, hope you like it or I'm sunk)
With this poem that is called –
(clap clap)
SLAM DUNK.

Handbagged

The flight was called. We were on our way
To our Greek island holiday.
Gate 23. He smiled at me.
Then suddenly I realised,
Not with what you'd call surprise,
More shock and awe –
As if a favourite pet had died,
Or England had failed to score –
My handbag was in my hand no more.
My bag! It's gone! I cried out loud,
Without a thought for all the crowd
Who were listening as they passed.

Is that important, then? he asked.
Important? I replied.
It's got my passport and my iPhone,
Ibuprofen, eyedrops, comb;
My tickets, out and home.
Money. Cards, debit and credit –
Oh where on earth could I have left it?
My diary and my notebook, my driving licence and my favourite pen!

Oh, he said. *Quite important, then.*
What? I screamed, like a bonfire night rocket.
Don't you understand?

Not really, he said. *I have pockets.*
Was there anything else in it?

A lottery ticket! Suppose that I win it!
That would be my kind of luck.
Chewing gum, toothpick, sweets to suck during take-off,
Which by the way is in twenty-five minutes..
Tissues and pills, a mirror, some bills,
Car keys, a torch, khaki shorts, spare pants,
All marked clearly with my name,
Stuff for killing bugs and ants; a game,
The poem that would one day be my only claim to fame;
My lucky charm and the little book of calm,
Which I could really do with now.

And, acting as if he didn't care.
He said, *I wondered what you kept in there,*

I carry my life in that bag!
My Swiss army knife, and a Leatherman tool,
A collapsible stool;
An oxy-acetylene torch so that if we crash land
I can cut a way out,
And a bucket of sand in case there's a fire..
All my worry and doubt,
And a small roll of wire.
A vodka and tonic, with lemon and ice;
A packet of rice – we might go to a wedding;
Buttons and safety pins, needle and thread –
And before you ask, no, not a spare bed.
Just clean bedding. A light quilt;
And a lifetime of guilt, my gambles, lost bets, successes, regrets,
Moments of elation, various means of sedation,
All my consonants and vowels, not to mention a towel –
I've read the Hitch-Hiker's Guide.

Don't panic, he replied.
You mean you've got all that inside one small bag?
Where does it all go?
And no kitchen sink?

Don't be stupid! I do have a plug, though.
But think, please think! What on earth can we do?
What's wrong with you?
You're behaving as if you don't mind!

Then he laughed at me. *I think you will find,*
He said, with a smirk, *that you've left behind*
The everyday bag that you use when you work,
And everything is actually safely on track –
All you need is in that big black rucksack
Which, I notice, is still on your back.
Calm down, dear. Let's go catch our flight.

Don't you just hate it when men are right?

Have you been?

Have you been? This mantra, three words long
Sticks in my mind like a persistent song –
It's how every journey started, in my youth.
And to tell the truth, I always had –
The alternative was just so bad;
Public loos were such a bother,
Because I was trained (and I bet I'm not the only one here) to hover –
Or at least apply
Carpets of bog roll, stacked up high.
If bum touched seat, my mum asserted,
Dread disease could not be averted –
Though exactly what was not made clear:
My mum would never say *gonorrhoea*.
But other bottoms were just unclean.
So – I made sure that I'd always been.

But this Harpic harping, I came to hate
'Cause it left me in a pathological state,
Unable even to contemplate
Using any loo that was not my own.
It was like Niagara when I got home.
And this continued until I was 48!
A success in other parts of life –
Businesswoman, mother, wife;
Confident that I would not fail.
I was a match for any male –
I could do all that they could do,
And I never spent any time in lieu.

Until at last I went away
On a walking tour, a holiday
Up in the hills, eight hours a day.
And lo! it came to pass
That I found the joy
Of crouching down behind a bush
And watering the grass.
As happy as any carefree boy,
With just a little privacy,
I could wee! It was an epiphany.

And now – well, frankly, I don't care,
Not a tittle or a jot.
I'll spend a penny anywhere,
In hole or porcelain or pot
I'll sit or squat,
Not minding where I piddle.
I've found the answer to my mum's Jimmy riddle.

Except recently, on one occasion,
In a very specific situation –
South Wales; a traffic jam; five hours long.
And all around me, a masculine throng,
Struck with the unforgiving urge,
Left their cars, made for the verge,
Turned their backs and found relief;
While I held on, beyond belief.
Boy was I jealous, was I green –
They were where I could have been
If I'd been born a man!
And now at last I understand.
It was a cruel sexist mockery,
All this blatant hand-on-cockery;
Yes, it was on the A478 to Tenby
That I learned what is meant by penis envy.
And it's not that I would want a willy -
I am a woman and that would be silly -
But I'd never have had to listen to all my mother's rants
If I could just take the piss without taking off my pants.

Bert and me

I've got a friend who's a heretic. Bert.
His heresy is quite specific –
He thinks the recession is terrific.
He says the whole capitalist system's rotten,
And should be swept aside and forgotten.
He comes from Stroud.

Well, I said to him, *people like you,*
You just don't think things through –
How would we buy stuff?
We'd swap, Bert said, *like they used to do.*
Money wouldn't be allowed.
Trade and barter, exchange and mart, a
Ban on cards and plastic.
We'd learn that resources aren't elastic.
And – he went on - *the multinational corporations would be*
            smashed to the ground,
Which we'd till and plough and sow and reap until we'd found
The level of subsistence appropriate for a sustained existence,
An economy based on agronomy;
And we, the pinnacle of creation would discover the true civilisation
That the natural world has to offer!
Bert's a bit of a philosopher.
But I work at the hospital, see;
Cancer unit; oncology.
The courage of those patients makes me weep.
And their treatments – well, they don't come cheap,
Gadalinium doesn't grow on trees,
And you can't knit them things that do endoscopies.
And if the world was run Bert's way,
Where would they come from? Who would pay?

So, I said to him, *Excuse me,* I said,
But you can't cobble together a positron emission tomography scanner
            in a garden shed,
And I don't care what you think –
No-one ever cooked up a batch of herceptin in a kitchen sink.
However well-scrubbed.
I could see I'd rubbed Bert up the wrong way.
For the first time since I've known him he didn't know what to say,

So I pushed my point home. *So what should we do then?*
I suppose you'd let them all die.

That the whole world might have everlasting life! was his reply.
What, like God gave his only son? I cried,
Or the coalition – they believe in sacrifice.
Other people's.
Now, I probably shouldn't have said that; it wasn't very nice,
And he does care about humanity, Bert,
But me, I just see people, and I didn't want him to be hurt,
So I added: *Not that I've got any answers – that's for sure.*
But you know what? Bert, my heretic friend–
Well, he don't seem to like me any more.

But that's ok. It's a price I'm prepared to pay,
Because I've had to listen to his rants on far too many occasions,
And to be frank, my sympathies lie with the patients
And the doctors who are trying to help the dying and the sick;
And I don't think Bert can see past the end of his... nose.

Starbucks
I could have written a poem about poverty and war;
Showed my mettle firing lines of military metaphor;
Or had a pop at politicians – they're always easy meat,
And George Bush impersonisationisms used to go down a treat.
I could have written a love poem, let you glimpse erotic bliss
And you would weep with unrequited passion, sigh and cry and kiss
And embrace the man sat next to you, or the woman – it's your choice.
I could ask you to participate – ok, when I say the word voice
       I'd like you all to shout out YES; let's try it now, crowd –
VOICE (*yes*)
       I meant out loud – VOICE (*YES*)...
I could ask you to participate and help you find your voice (*YES*) –
But it's just to make you feel involved, I'll willingly confess.
I could include a chorus that's repeated now and then.
I could include a chorus that's repeated now and then,
But my favourite trick's the little bit where I begin to sing –
Something you will recognise, though not *the real thing;*
And quoting from an advert might get you on my side –
We'd smugly share the thought that we're not taken for a ride.

I could spit bitter bile about relationships with men,
And I could include a chorus that's repeated now and then.
Perhaps I'd swear a little bit, show I don't give a f-f-f-ig,
And say: contains explicit lyrics (in letters *this* big).
I could cry woe for global warming, show I really care,
Though I'm not sure if it helps at all to add still more hot air.
I could gripe about globalisation, Starbucks and the rest –
Check out your social conscience – would you pass the Nestlé test?

But – the coffee chains are popular 'cause they make a tasty brew,
But these percolated verses strain the life that's filtered through –
We're not here for espresso, nothing deep and dark and strong:
Even mocha is too macho – please tell me if I'm wrong.
These are skinny latte couplets, frothy feelings, poetry lite –
I'm a cappuccino poet here to whip your cream tonight,
And I'll serve you with a smile and a decaffeinated pen –
Though I might include a chorus that's repeated now and then.

But all anger is just artificial creamer in our sounds –
A tepid frappé fury, which hasn't any grounds.
We manipulate emotions, although we know it sucks.
Yes, we're all in the gutter, but some people see Starbucks
And they go there 'cause they like it; but we know what we're here for,
So we save the proper poems for the winner's last encore,
And the rest is titillation when there's nothing real to say –
Just oral stimulation 'cause we daren't go all the way,
And whoever makes you clap and cheer, they're hoping
        that you'll know
That inside's a Fairtrade poet, shouting – *Please! This one! To go!*

Rather drink

I've been thinking
That if I were one of those people who got
        a lot of pleasure from booze, then every weekend I'd
        be out drinking.

I would down Rum and Coke and Sex on the Beach
        and Long Hard Screws and all those other drinks
        with silly names,
And think it a great achievement to win drinking games.

And when the barman said, *I think we might have had*
        enough now, madam, and asked me to leave,
I would find it hard to believe,
And insist on just one more,
And not quite understand that offering to bite off
        someone's left ear means, usually,
        that you find yourself on the other side of the door,
Plus bruises
In places where no-one, sober, chooses.

I'd be one of those people you see in real-life cop shows,
        throwing up in the middle of Swindon
With gay abindon.
I would laugh at nothing
        and put my arms round my friends
        with no embarrassment,
And complain of police harassment
When they tried to stop me walking round
        wearing nothing but a traffic cone
And took me home.

And although, like every drunk,
        when I woke the next morning with
        an M1 full of road-building equipment
        working (far more than they ever do on the M1)
        in my head,
And would leave my bed
Only to worship at the loo's altar,
And say, *Never again!* I would do this
        in the knowledge that this vow would certainly falter,
Because it would only be when I'm on a binge
That I could stop the Swindon of my life,
        the M1 of each tarmac day,
        from making me cringe,
And whinge, and cry.
I'd rather drink, and sooner die.

Damaged goods
Sometimes, a new love appears
Like something ordered through the mail:
Taut, shiny, perfectly packed,
Ready to be attacked
With passion, wrapping ripped
Away, as you burrow
For the prize within,
Ignoring polystyrene worms
(The germs of what might follow).
You wallow in the newness,
Delight in the strange twoness
Of it all.

But we – we are
Two parcels with addresses lost,
Tape torn, edges worn
And tattered;
Waiting as if hope mattered;
Pre-owned, secondhand,
Slightly used, previously enjoyed –
With all the unsureness
Of threeness or fourness
Behind us;
Expectations meagre;
No longer eager,
But wary, shivery
With anxiety, not ardour;
Not knowing if we should
Reject delivery of each other
Or try, just that bit harder, to accept these
Damaged goods.

But it's not only that we both have baggage –
Histories and mysteries and pasts –
It's not just our souls that are damaged:
Human bodies were not meant to last.
And my face has been cross-hatched by some mad cartoonist;
My bum's only ogled by hot-air balloonists –

It all makes me squirm
And the one thing that's firm
Is my long-term belief
That some thief (opportunist)
Has stolen my beautiful youth.

Oh yes, I may try some misguided disguise –
Black lycra pants conceal orange-peel thighs,
Grey hair erased by l'Oreal dyes
(Because I'm worth it!)
But nothing can quite hide the truth.
And, well, as for you,
I know you can't chew
Until you remove that one false front tooth.
Hair spurts from your ears instead of your crown;
You run out of breath on a stroll into town;
You can't see your toes unless you sit down –
Time touches each part as it passes;
And both of us need to wear glasses.
But I can read your heart, and it's not in bad shape,
So before arthritis prevents our escape
From this cold isolation in bubble-wrap limbo
Love, please be my squeeze, and I'll be your bimbo!
So we've been here before – we can try it once more;
Let's open the box, and to hell with Pandora;
We're perfectly matched; we should act with despatch –
After so long in transit there's no strings attached,
And no postage due – I was sent just for you!
And time's running out. Without further ado
Remove my plain wrapper – it's rescue, not rape -
Just take care as you peel off my old sellotape;
But sign to accept, don't return me to sender –
Be mine (on approval) – and I'll be
          Yours, Brenda.

Games

I am in love with a man who plays games.
Rick, I call him now, though, sadly, Eric is his name.
It started more or less with a simple game of chess.
I knew I wouldn't win – I was an absolute beginner –
But my strategy for this date was that we might be moved to mate.
The conclusion was foregone; but I didn't feel forlorn
When I pondered on the pun, indeed the homophonic
Quite symbolic meaning of – the pawn.
And the evening had only just begun.

He said *Now we'll have some fun.*
D'you want Monopoly or Cluedo, snakes and ladders or Perudo?
Well, you don't find sexy laughs in a quiet game of draughts.
And what I had in mind was an erotic kind of judo,
Scarcely Scrabble, more strip ludo;
But it wasn't very long before we moved on to Mah Jong,
Though my thoughts were not of dragons, but his pung against
             my kuong.

Then came trivial pursuit, which just didn't toot my flute;
My interests weren't quizzical – I wanted to get physical,
I needed to be kissed, not deal a hand at knock-out-whist;
And pick-up-sticks don't flick my switch -
I was really getting pissed.
Off.
It had all become absurd;
Eric definitely was a nerd;
And then he started up again, with some paper and a pen.
Dammit, let the man go hang! I cried. *I don't want snap, but bang!*
And it's time I had my say – why not have a go at rôle play?

Now, I was in a slam one night – some other poet won,
But as a booby prize I got the outfit of a nun.
(And that's absolutely true!)
The change was swiftly done, but things didn't seem complete
Till Eric turned his collar round and put sandals on his feet;
We improvised a cassock from my best black satin sheet.

And it really did the trick, as if he'd thrown a double six.
His finesse was smoother, slicker, his responses so much quicker,
Snapped elastic in my knickers; and we never even bicker
'Cause now we know what game to play since that orgasmic, epic day,
When Eric the prick in a tick became Rick who gets kicks
           kitting up as a vicar!

Playa del Ingles

The old couple on holiday went to the beach, and sat down
           to look at the boats.
They had food wrapped in foil, and suntan oil, and, of course,
           their light summer coats.
Then something wobbly caught Dad's eye, and he exclaimed to Ma,
By 'eck, what are those – and look at that bum; ee,
           who do they think they are?

For they had strayed onto the nudist part of the beach at
           Playa del Ingles,
And all around was the sight and sound of a group of naked singles.
Then Ma sat upright, with full view of a sight that made her cheeks
           burn so hot –
Quick, look at that man with the teak-effect tan – there's
           a ring through the end of his I-don't-know-what!

But after a while they started to smile at what they could still remember
Of when passion burned bright as Canarian sun, and was not
           just a glowing ember;
As if in a dream they thought back to a stream, on a
           warm August night , '53;
And exchanging a glance, they accepted this chance, and
           they stood and with some dignity
They stripped to the skin, without saying a thing, and hand in hand,
           skipped to the sea.

Robot

I fell in love with a roboteer –
A man who could mould aluminium and steel;
He knew how to fettle, fought battles with metal.
I thought I would teach him to feel.

How could there be glitches? He flicked all my switches –
Wired me up, turned me on, made me go.
He awoke all my urges with powerful surges;
His digital skills meant my current could flow

And our physical fusion was like molten solder;
With a tongue tense as tungsten he tickled and teased;
He had perfect hydraulics! I gave up my Horlicks
And spend my nights glowing with his LEDs.

And soon I was moving to all his commands –
No capacity left for resistance or shame.
He had total control – but where was his soul?
I was only a tool in his new hand-held game,

For despite my devotion, he felt no emotion.
What about love? I would ask now and then.
He smiled back, all laconic: *It's just electronic,*
He said, and he told me again and again:
We're nothing but a bunch of ions.

And I thought,
What the fuck is he talking about?
Irons are hot things with steam sprays;
You use them to get rid of creases…
But – my passions were ceaseless, I still had no doubt,
Not even when he said, *Sit still, this might sting,*
And under my ear – can you see it? Just here? –
He inserted a chip – and only he knew the pin,

And he painted me silver, from forehead to feet;
And he dyed my hair gold (though I do like it blonde);
Electrodes were stowed on my toes, up my nose –
And inside other places that nobody knows.
His remote control worked like a weird wizard's wand.

He took me to all the robot conventions,
Displayed me – his consummate act of creation.
This unfeeling geek made me jump, jerk and squeak –
A triumph of high-tech android animation
But
For me it was nothing but humiliation;

For this is how all my relationships go –
I give all I have; my self-esteem's tiny;
I let myself change at the hands of male strangers –
Though my skin doesn't usually get polished and shiny...

I had given him everything – heart, body, mind;
He'd converted me into a robotic alien
With analogue rape. I planned my escape –
This was to be Frankenstein's tale, not Pygmalion;
So one night, in my armour, I took up his tools,
And I spot welded him - where the sun doesn't shine.
He awoke with a shriek and struggled to speak:
I wanted to make sure you'd always be mine!

Then he uttered no more, and I thought I was free –
I was human and female and not a machine.
But though he's dead and gone, his spirit lives on,
And is still relayed through me in infra-red dreams,
And it makes my limbs stutter, my heart go a-flutter
When I hear about science – fiction or true:
I find Star Trek exotic, Stephen Hawking erotic,
And I come to a climax when I watch Doctor Who!

COCABOG

Cheese 'n' onion crisps and a bottle of ginger beer.
Already, from the back, not surprisingly, I hear
Murmurs of unrest: *What the hell's that got to do with Hallowe'en?*
I will explain. I'll do my best. I'll set the scene.
Long, long ago in a city far, far away –
London, the early sixties, when everything was grey,
Even the hazy pictures on the television screen –
Black and white my behind!
Nothing so precise, so well-defined.
But we were very nice, and so refined.
Not in our wildest dreams would we have thought of trick or treat.
Mugging poor old ladies for a biscuit or a sweet?
You must be joking!
We thought we'd won a prize poking diamond holes for eyes
        in scraggy pumpkins.
But I was a timid child, and knew my place;
Couldn't even look a pumpkin in the face.
They were so – pierced. And fierce. Grrr.
Just like the Hallowe'en kids today –
They roam the streets dressed up, red make-up dripping
From their lips, clearly tripping on Red Bull,
But all we had was apple-bobbing: dipping under water for a nibble
Of a Cox's orange pippin! If we were lucky.

Anyway. That particular Hallowe'en,
My parents decided I had grown
Enough to be left on my own.
For the very first time. Home, alone.
While they went to a party.
Are you sure you'll be all right? Oh, here,
We bought you these for company, dear –
Cheese 'n' onion crisps and a bottle of ginger beer.

I'll be fine! I simpered.
The door closed, and I whimpered as I turned on the TV.
A film. Werewolf in London was what the evening held for me.
I was in London. And it's scarier in black and white;
When you're on your own; on Hallowe'en night.

I took a drink, and gurgled,
Waiting to be burgled
By a horde of blood-starved vampires dying for a bite.
Crisps, then. The packet crackled,
And I could hear the witches cackle, and I couldn't tackle them –
I was too little for a fight!
Outside the bats were flying, and the ghouls and ghosties vying
To be first to slip within with the imps and will-o'-the-wisps,
And they wanted *me*, never mind the flaming drink or sodding crisps!
And then – the devil came in the room. I couldn't hide;
       I watched him crawl,
Getting nearer, and nearer, high above me on the wall…
Ok, it was a spider; but it was very, very big and I wasn't tall
Enough to catch it or to kill it. Will it get me?
My stomach churned with fear, as I slurped my ginger beer,
Turned the bottle upside down. I just couldn't seem to stop
Until I'd drained the fiery fizz down to the final flaming drop.
And I knew trouble was brewing, when in a frenzy, without chewing,
I swallowed crisps in handfuls till I was full up to the top,
And I don't even like cheese 'n' onion!

Then I was sick. All over the rug.
I started to recover. With a smile and a shrug,
I took myself to bed, contented that my mother
And my dad deserved this gift
For being mean on Hallowe'en,
And going off to party, leaving me to face my fear
With nothing but cheese 'n' onion crisps and a bottle of ginger beer.

Dubya

January 2009 will see the end of an era.
Despite his years concerned with our security,
A world leader will pass into well-earned obscurity.
The time grows nearer,
So let us here today
Pay tribute with just some of the words
That we have heard him say.

I know the human being and fish can coexist peacefully.
I don't need to explain things. I believe what I believe is right.
I trust that God speaks through me. Without that, I could not do my job.
The most important job is not to be governor, or first lady in my case.
It's a struggle between good, and it's a struggle between evil.
They said, you know, this issue doesn't resignate with people.
We're in a culture of moral indifference, tolerance touted as
          a great virtue.
For every fatal shooting, there were roughly three non-fatal,
And, folks, this is unacceptable. And we're gonna
          do something about it.
(We're making the right decisions to bring the solution to an end.)
I know the human and fish can being peacefully coexist.

If you're sick of the politics of principle, come and join this campaign.
We don't need any more theory in Washington. We need people that
          actually done.
We look forward to hearing your vision so we can more better
          do our job.
I recognize there are hurdles, and we're going to achieve those hurdles.
I can press where there needs to be pressed; hold hands
          where there needs to be – hold hands.
I'm surprised at the amount of distrust that exists, and I'll
          work hard to elevate it.
You can fool some of the people all the time, and these are
          the ones to concentrate on.
You couldn't make it up, could you?
The human being can fish I know and peacefully coexist.

Take border relations between Canada and Mexico –
      they've never been better.
But the thing that's wrong with the French is they have no word
      for entrepreneur.
This foreign policy stuff is a little frustrating.
An Iraq that can govern, sustain itself is more than a military mission,
And that's precisely the reason why I sent more troops into Baghdad.
We cannot let terrorists hold this nation hostile, or hold
      our allies hostile.
Our enemies are resourceful, and never stop thinking of new ways
To harm our country and our people. And neither do we.
If America goes to sleep, the rest of the world is in trouble.
You've aroused a compassionate nation, and we're going to
      hunt you down.
Success is not no violence. It's a death that we can heal.
Fish can coexist peacefully, and I know the human being.

I just want you to know – when we talk about war, we're really
      talking about peace.
They misunderestimated me. I want to be the peace president.
I'm like any political figure; everybody wants to be loved.
Wisdom and strength and my family is what I'd like you to pray for.
Families is where our nation finds hope – where wings take dream.
(I want to thank you for taking time to come and witness my hanging.)
Peacefully being the human fish, I can know and coexist.
Does that make any sense to you? It's kind of muddled.
In my sentences I go where no man has gone before.
Can I know the fish peacefully? And being human, coexist?

I coexist? Fish peacefully? You know? Just can it, human beings.

Glad rags

It is a commonplace, a fact held self-evidently true,
That, in poetry at least, sad is easiest to do,
And to write a happy poem far more hard.
Well, I don't feel much like challenges; scarred
By attacks of memories twenty times a day,
From confidential coffee-cups, a word they used to say,
The intimacies of clothing, a startling song – I play
A game now, counting the *remember me?* blows,
And the score of reminiscence hits just grows;
And I recoil from recall though God knows
I don't want to forget –
Not yet, not yet.

So I'm not ready now to wear the glad rags of a jester;
Until I lance this sorrow with sad words the wounds will fester
And take far more time to heal.
It is no crime to feel
This way,
So if I'm far away
And for a while I can't amuse you,
Please be patient; it would be wrong for me to use you
As a jocular comfort when the pain
Belongs elsewhere. Please complain,
If you wish, at the sadness of the song,
But I can't lie with laughter; memories go on too long;

For this is how it is when kids are taken by their father.
We often hear of the pain of absent dads – but think now, rather,
Of the sorry state of being of that rare breed, the absent mother,
Whose other
Half sees fit to kit their kids in clothes of anger and mistrust,
Who thinks it right to teach them that they must
No longer love the one who fed them,
Who gladly read them
Stories every night,
And with a child's delight led them
To discoveries of life.

How satisfying for him to twist this savage knife;
How pleasing it must be, this manipulation
Of mere children, switching their adulation
To himself; how sweet the power,
Knowing every hour
Of every day of every week of every year,
I have and do and will weep tears
Of loss, breathe sighs of grieving;
And the sharp anguish of the leaving
Is a tiny insect sting
Compared with the continuing
Rat-bites of reminders each day holds.
I hope he relishes his dish of revenge, not only eaten cold,
But never-ending. Please complain,
If you wish, at the sadness of this song,
But I can't lie with laughter; my memories go on too long.

Free radicals
(*Pour three glasses of wine , drink one, and start second*)
Three glasses of red wine a day,
Is what my doctor had to say -
They would without doubt keep at bay
All furring of the arteries,
And help my beating heart, which is
Getting older as we speak;
And put an end to the steady leak
Into my bloodstream of those bad little
Things called free radicals,
Which would otherwise oxidise my cells –
That's what the doc said, and he seems well,
And for something you like to be good is quite magical -
And it's more fun than being dead. *(drink half of second glass)*

But the doctor's words seemed slightly absurd -
So I looked up radical in the dictionary:
Proponent of total reform; revolutionary.
Now I might be pedantic, semantically -
But I worshipped Che Guevara, romantically;
I've got a soft spot for radicals, me,
And I really believe they ought to be free.

Don't get me wrong; it's no forgive-me ticket;
I know I should think capitalism's wicked,
But I just admire old Trotsky's spirit –
Though wine's the drink I use;   *(finish second)*
But if I had a chance to choose,
I would release all my radicals!
(As long as they haven't got hammers and sickles).

(Pour third glass)
But did my doctor actually look at me?
I'm not very big, as you can see,
And after just a glass and a half
I start to giggle and laugh
And, er, lose the thread of what I was saying and I just sort of ramble on
and never reach the end of a sentence or a verse,
And what's worse,   *(start third)*
I really start needing a pee.   *(drink more of 3rd)*

Oh. I'm not sure about this.
I'm definitely feeling a little bit pissed,
And that's when I stray into phisolophy,
After the wine and before the coffee;
And the big question here, it seems to me,
Is - like lunch, can there logically be
A radical who is truly free?
Not if you ask me!
Cheers!
(finish last glass)

Survival of the fruitiest

In my earliest days as a poet I was invited to join in a group –
Though I guess it was more of a gang, a platoon,
      an aggressive performing troupe;
We spouted poems in pubs and cafés and bars,
In banks and in barbers', museums, parked cars –
And our victims could never predict our attack;
Against terrorist poets they tried to fight back;
But with meter for mortars, each sonnet a bomb it
Was fun to run into the flak.

We christened ourselves the guerrillas –
Che Guevara had nothing on us!
As covert couplet killers
It gave us a thrill as
We haiku'd the queue for the bus.

We had poems on politics, chocolate and sex,
And drinking and thinking and sport;
On passion and pain, love, and sex once again –
We thought people should know what we thought.

But we weren't from some up-itself university –
Our origins showed a wide-ranging diversity:
With knowledge of nations, advanced computations,
Christianity, profanity, public relations,
We had vanity, insanity, and bad reputations –
Everyone thought we were strange;
And then it all started to change

We began to look into the laws of genetics
Which govern the world's evolution;
Our attempts at reform seemed puny, pathetic -
A rondeau redoublé however poetic
Would not bring about revolution.

We found fascination in facts of creation,
And how other species behave,
Because with the apes, our nearest relations
('Cause man's just a monkey that's learned how to shave)
We share 98.8% of our genes

75

Which means
That the odd 1.2, we can safely infer,
Are what cause qualms of conscience on wearing real fur.
And – we're 80 percent like iguanas.
But what struck us all mute was our closeness to fruit –
We are two-fifths the same as bananas.

We abandoned our image as metaphor killers;
Became furry, and friendly, and simply, gorillas.
And here's the moral of this tale -
We can all make this earth more like heaven;
More peaceful and happy and calmer;
Don't use words to threaten like AK47s –
Just unzip your inner banana!

Substitute

Dear Santa,
        For Christmas, I don't want nothing smelly,
And none of those things advertised on the telly.
I don't want no necklace or bracelet or ring,
Or minute sexy undies that are no more than string.
I don't want no gadgets for cooking or cleaning,
Or daft little books, full – they say – of deep meaning.
I'm not keen on music, so please no CDs,
And I still haven't watched last year's DVDs.
I'd get fat on chocolates, so don't bring me those,
And my wardrobes are bursting – I don't want no clothes.

But I think you should know that one thing is missing.
Where my mistletoe hangs there's a space good for kissing,
But there's only me in it, with no-one to hold,
And though I'm dressed up warm, inside I'm all cold.
So Santa, I'm begging you, please, if you can,
Don't need wrapping or ribbons – just send me a man!

P.S.
There are twelve days of Christmas – would one be enough?
After so long without, things could get pretty rough,
So to be on the safe side, I think what would suit
Would be a whole football team – plus substitute.

In praise of men

I wouldn't like to shave each day,
With that perennial decision –
Will I be less of a man, will I face the world's derision
If I use fewer blades than four?
I wouldn't like to worry as I got near any door –
If I let a woman go through first, will she see it as demeaning,
Or know that I'm well-meaning and polite?
I wouldn't like to feel that every night
I must slump senseless on the sofa,
Seize control of the remote, and just loaf a-
Round and watch tv,
In the hope that I'll find something I can curse about.
I wouldn't like to have only two topics to converse about –
No, on second thoughts, make that three –
When Top Gear and first-team tactics pall, well, there's always sex,
As long as it's all conquest and no passion.
When I met other men, I'd hate to expect
To take part in dick wrestling, just to win respect.
I wouldn't like to dress merely for comfort and not fashion.
But hang on; you know what? Actually, I would;
That's one aspect of being a man that's really rather good.
I wouldn't want to risk rejection
Every time I see a girl I like.
It's one thing facing rational objections,
But there's no appropriate response, I think, to "On yer bike!"
At times of deep emotion, I wouldn't want to joke,
'Cause if I shed a tear, I wouldn't be a proper bloke.
I wouldn't want her cold feet up against me when I'm warm.
I wouldn't like that pressure to perform,
That two-faced *understanding* if some nights I couldn't make it.
I wouldn't like the fact that it's impossible to fake it.
I wouldn't like the helplessness when there's something to be found;
I wouldn't want to always have to put the loo seat down –
Why shouldn't women leave it up? –
Or the suspicion that the family only want to have me round
For heavy lifting, shifting furniture and so on.
I can go on.
I wouldn't want to wear a tie; I wouldn't want to be relied upon.
I wouldn't want to take the blame for almost anything you can name;
I wouldn't want the heaviness of being a big brother.

I wouldn't want to know that I could never be a mother.
I wouldn't want to know that there are women who would think of me
        as little more than a potential rapist,
As a power-crazed and dominating sadist,
As a lazy hapless slob, and nothing more.
I wouldn't want the job of fighting wars.

I sing a song in praise of men,
Who carefully hide their feelings when
We women whinge, complain and groan.
The happy pangs of childbirth give no just cause to moan;
They are nothing to the handicaps of being a *mere male*.
I wouldn't like to be a man, 'cause I'm fairly sure I'd fail.

Power
There's no greater power any minute, any hour
Than the power of the word; the power of the word.
You'll be shaken and stirred, fly free as a bird
Tell me what you've heard – it's the power of the word.

It gives power to the old and the very very young;
You've known it since you first said *Mama w*hen you were just one –
It's the power of the word – the first thing that you heard –
The power of the word.

It can make you strong; it can make you free
It can turn you into anything you'll ever want to be
It's the power of the word; the power of the word.

Now you tell me what you've heard
It's the power of the
The power of
The power
The
It's the power, the power,
The earth-quaking, mind-shaking,
War-breaking, peace-making
Yours for the taking
Power
Of the word!

Hero

Even at fifty, you are the hero.
Burning buildings, runaway trains, sinking ships, terrorised planes –
The lot.
Me, I am the dope, sitting watching with my mouth open,
While you make sure only bad guys get things broken,
And you know what?
I've never even got my vest dirty,
Partly because it's pink and slinky and a little bit flirty;
But you are up and down those elevator shafts
Like a rat in a sewer.
Definitely a doer, a mover and a shaker.
When earthquakes rumble,
You're in like Flynn,
Chasing those giant worms.
When volcanoes grumble,
Last out is your turn,
Hardly raising a lather while racing lava.
When skyscrapers tumble,
You're the risk-taker, who goes where only Dan dares.
You're always there when things get hot,
Despite your creaky joints and liver spots,
And the lines on your face deeper than the San Andreas fault,
Which you could probably halt single-handed.
Ok, to be candid
You are a bit of a heartbreaker,
Largely because you are too busy saving other people's lives
To look after you wives, who sometimes die.
But you never cry,
Just bite your lip and mumble a bit,
And carry on being the same old shit
Where personal relationships are concerned.
Me, I've throbbed and yearned,
Not to be your love interest, such as it is;
No. I want to be you.
Not cocooned in my semi-detached three-bedroomed nest,
Safe in a dress. I long to possess
And wear that vest,
With its gradually increasing mess of blood and mud.

And God, I've prayed for jets to crash land in my back garden,
For my back yard to erupt,
My next door neighbour to be the corrupt
Politician, nasty as Nero,
Who gets his in the second reel,
And for me to be the hero!
I know just how it would feel;
I've lived through it often enough.
I know things might get tough
And some will die; but not me –
I'll walk free, just bruised and grazed
And grubby, knife in one hand, rescued puppy
In the other. That'll show my mother,
Who raised me as a girlie, but always loved my brother more.
I'm prepared for a bit of rough, with reality unsteady;
I'm ready even for aliens,
And they can be swift and sure, quick on the draw, and nifty.
But it's you, you who are the hero,
Even at fifty.
Ah, Bruce, Steven, Ed, Harrison, Sly – why
Not I? Why can't I have a go?
But deep inside I know
I could never get out of your kind of trouble
Without direction, lighting, continuity, costume, make-up and music
And the money to pay for a good stunt double.
No. I'm the dope, watching with my mouth open,
All hopes broken, 'cause it's much too late
For me to cheat death and/or fate or even debt,
And there's nothing I can do,
Because Hollywood hasn't called me yet,
And I'm even older than you.

Nuts

I bought some intimate lubricant – nothing wrong with that,
      don't panic.
The packet claimed it was Fairtrade, vegetarian and organic.
Now, when you reach a certain age, mornings are the best.
Everything works better when you've had a good night's rest.
So, we wanted to get slippery, on that fateful morning.
That's when I read the small print, with this vague, unsettling warning:
Product made in a facility where the workers may have handled nuts.
And I thought, whose? Do they get a chance to choose?
Is that how they test this stuff? And suddenly, I'd had enough.
Now, I once did philosophy – I was an ethics girl –
And this subject means a lot to me. My thoughts began to whirl.
Now, girls, I'm sure you'll understand. Sex can be all-consuming,
But sometimes you're distracted by, e.g., his personal grooming,
Or lack thereof; or if you've got any ironed clothes to wear.
Things like that. He was putting the effort in, but my mind
      was off elsewhere,
Anyway. We'd started so we finished, but I couldn't concentrate.
Being told to base my life on fear is something that I hate.
So I missed the post-orgasmic bliss, that fluffy soft meringue.
Instead, I sat up straight in bed, and launched on a harangue.
We have the right to hurt ourselves! The thinking is quite clear.
We can smoke or go hang-gliding, or drown ourselves in beer.
If you turn on the hot tap, then the water will be hot;
If you buy a bag of peanuts, then peanuts is what you've got!
Why swallow junior Calpol, which is meant for under-fives,
If you operate machinery, or you're planning a long drive?
What is this life if, full of care, we only dare to stand and stare?
By now my rage had made me stand, though my poor bloke
      was still seated.
I heard him mutter: *Caution – this speaker might get heated.*
He seemed a little angry now, but I was in full swing.
Why tell me that this fish has bones? I can choke on anything!
If I want to.
If we don't have any danger, there isn't any hope.
We must stop this senseless nannying, which has broadened out
      its scope:
Breast milk gives the best protection for your baby, croons the tube.
Well, not if there's a car crash, when an airbag beats a boob.

And on I went, and on and on, and on and on and on.
He'd dressed by now, ready to leave, and my voice was nearly gone,
But I managed one strong parting shot – I'll put in some asterisks –
For when he waved, he said *Take care!*
And I said, *Haven't you f***ing heard a f***ing word? Don't take care*
  – take risks!
But I haven't seen him since, and I've begun to change my mind.
At my age, a steady weekly f-f-friend is really hard to find.
I should have kept my mouth shut. There are no ifs or buts.
Sometimes *take care* is good advice, if you want to handle nuts.

Witchcraft on his lips
Shakespeare talked of a woeful ballad,
written to a mistress' eyebrow;
well, I could write one now about the eyebrow of my lover:
it sits above his eye like a rainbow in the sky,
only furry and dark brown, like a beard turned upside down,
or a caterpillar creeping, arching its hairy back.
It's a shame the other one doesn't match;
he has an asymmetric frown, and his smile is quite unnerving.
Still, it's well worth while observing
that he's tall and strong and wants to share my life,
so I guess I should forgive the funny way he holds his knife –
does he think he's *writing* dinner?
But he's good-looking and he's slim,
and I've always like men on the thinner side,
and he's never ever lied to me,
and women soon learn to ignore
the worst bad dream of all – the way men snore –
so I'll refrain from pouring scorn
upon that honk, that grunt, that loud foghorn –
a jug of water in the night does well enough, I find.
And he's courteous, and very kind, and treats me like a lady,
and you'd think maybe this thing could grow.
This thing, I said; not his – size isn't everything you know,
as we quickly learn to say; although it is.
But I'm here to praise my man, not slag him off!
I'd *like* to keep him on, not pack him off,
But. The truth is, our relationship is heading straight for death,
because my boyfriend – and there's no easy way to say this –

82

oh, my boyfriend has bad breath.
It didn't really bother me the first time that we kissed:
garlic, curry, onions – any item on this list could be to blame,
but the smell was still the same on the second and the third occasion,
and by the fourth I'd come to the unhappy realisation
that this odour is part of him; it lies down in the heart of him;
and breathing through your mouth alone can only go so far –
I've even put a forest fragrance freshener in my car.
And I can forget the rest; the little quirks don't really matter.
I wouldn't even mind if he grew a little fatter,
but this witchcraft on his lips, this stink of sewers is too much.
I have to turn my back, though I'm longing for his touch;
and I can talk to him of eyebrows, knives and snoring and the rest,
but this – it's just too difficult to get it off my chest.
We'd rather die than be embarrassed – we all know this is true –
isn't it? would *you* say anything? or you? or you? or you?
And I've really done my best; dropped a hint – and mint – or two,
but let's face it – I'd feel better if I started sniffing glue.
I know love should be a fixèd star, that looks on tempests
       and is not shaken,
but I can't face this foul fume of sighs, every time I waken.
I can't compare him to a summer's day! The Bard's words
       came very pat,
but my boyfriend has bad breath, and Shakespeare
       never mentioned *that*.

Carbon footprint

It was a dark and stormy night!
Is the very worst way, so teachers say,
To start a story when you write;
But it's how my tale begins:
When lonely and abandoned by love's lies
I stood and stared at the wild night skies
Where fragile onion skins of cloud
Were peeled away by loud and hungry winds,
Revealed a moon, so angry and scary
That it daunted even hairy werewolves,
Taunted unwary poets robbed of timeworn imagery.
The stars were little more than livid scars
Of primordial savagery, bite marks on the night's firm flesh –
        but I digress.

Of all the constellations, there is only one I know:
Orion's Belt – they call it that, but really it's just three stars in a row;
But this night Orion stood aloft in ancient hunter's dress, his bow
Held high, arrow aimed at my tremulous eye,
And his voice shot to me from the sky:
You! Yes, you, with knuckles white, clutching at your clothes,
And shaking in your boots; yes, you, dyed hair, with roots
That need retouching! I have been sent by Zeus to say that you
Must mend your wasteful ways!

That was all he said, and, dazed, I went to bed,
And fantasized, caught in a haze of thought
Of Orion in his glory, warning me.
I woke to find it all had been a dream
(The very worst way to *end* a story – so I will go on.)
The storm had passed. I looked out at my garden.
There, on the grass, was a footprint, huge, scorched
In blackest carbon. Orion
Had left a sion.

Since then, I've tried so very hard.
I recycle cans and glass and card; no standby lights are allowed to glow;
The compost helps my veggies grow; the washing machine's
        turned down to thirty
(Which means my clothes always look a bit dirty);

I've resoled my shoes, there are bricks in the loos, I get my news from
the internet – not printed; my dedication's so unstinted that I've even
said tara to my car and found my way to the railway station and spent
fortunes on extortionate train fares allowing me to share my space with
hoi polloi who make a noise and soil the seats with their feet, pollute my
commute with mobile phone ring tones and don't know a thing about
Orion and don't buy in to the environment at all!

But I have the consolation that my attempts at conservation
            have proved fruitful.
My lawn once more is buitful. The carbon footprint's shrunk,
            become quite small.

But still my life seems empty, unfulfilled,
And I lean against my window sill,
Staring at night skies,
Swathed demurely in my nightie,
And wondering: have I not deserved the prize
Of being visited, once again,
By this handsome hunter,
This god among men –
But this time, please, on a mission
From Aphrodite?

Than this

Look. Please tell me what you see –
I'm not that bad for fifty-three!
Yes, gravity's dragged down my bum,
But I don't – yet – look like my mum;
Though names and stuff I do forget,
I haven't lost my marbles yet;
And I hold my own in company –
Some people *like* to be with me!
But you... need space.
With that faraway look on your face,
I want to be alone, you say;
We'll still talk on the phone, you say,
And firmly shut the door.
And this makes me feel just like a whore...

Everything I am, everything I have is yours,
But you withdraw within your cave, behave
As cavemen did, with a boulder lid
To hide behind.
Well, one day you'll peer out and find
Tigers of loneliness as neighbours,
With isolation's teeth, sharp sabres
To rip your guts and make you understand
What you have missed –
You could have been my man,
But you reject commitment's kiss,
And I'm worth more than this;
Yes, I'm worth more than this.

And I see outside, hear others' tears,
And touch the fears, and smell the noise,
And – well, I've worked with boys in prison cells –
Truc victims in a trainee hell,
With doors by others locked real tight
On furnaces of pain and fright;
A killing kiln
To sear their souls, and fire their minds,
Brand dotted slash lines on their wrists,
And turn them into whores for crime,
Give them false reasons to exist –

Well, they're worth more than this;
Yes, they're worth more than this.

And I must see all there is to see;
'Cause we all watch fake reality –
The immoral illegality
Of a teletubby horror game,
Where Orwell's nightmare haunts and lives
And we get what Big Brother gives –
A poisoned budget – fame for shame –
And captive kids are fucked and pissed
On gawping love and money's kiss;
Seduced, they are publicity's whores
As revenues roll, and ratings soar –
But they're worth more than this;
Yes, they're worth more than this.

And of all whores we're the dirtiest kind,
'Cause prostitutes don't sell their minds;
There's dignity in trading sex –
A job well done means self-respect.
But we're the lowest, feeblest whores,
For we let others fight our wars.
We ask no pay for our permission;
Abandon hope to politicians
Who'll beat poverty - from flashy cars.
We barely even raise a mutter,
Let alone a brave clenched fist –
Well, we're all in the gutter,
But some of us see stars,
And we know we can resist
Because we're worth more than this;
Yes, we're worth more than this.

And when you shut out the love I give
It wakes in me the need to live
And leap out of inaction's bed –
We'll sleep alone when we are dead;
Your space is all inside your head
So open your eyes and find your voice:
Gutter or stars – you have a choice,

And one day you'll know what you've missed
If you hide from commitment's kiss –
Because you're worth more than this!
Yes, you are worth more than this.

Sounds of science
When I would lay me down to sleep,
My thoughts would darken and grow deep;
I'd think of syzygy, infinity, gluons, cosmic strings;
Synapses and quarks – lot of scientific things
I could never comprehend; and drowsy in the dark I'd sing:
Hallo quarkness my old friend;
I am bemused by you again.
Because there was no vision softly creeping -
However hard I was peeping,
Minute particles weren't articles –
I couldn't touch them, smell them, see them.
How could I believe? I was a scientific heathen.
And in finding this a mystery I wasn't on my tod,
For biologists believe in chemistry,
Chemists believe in physics, and physicists just believe in god,
So for all their perfect beauty, for all their fearful symmetry,
Like everything I could not see – molecules, electricity -
These elements of science seemed just fairy tales to me.

But – I have a back tooth filling, of metallic shiny mercury,
And it's long picked up the signals from radio and TV.
But recently I've recognised its unique sonic quality –
It's playing, high-fidelity, guess what, that's right –
           the sounds of science.

Sssh! Listen carefully!
I can hear dark matter sing along with the strings in deep curved space;
On the moon the stars and stripes flaps flagging quietly in its place;
I can hear the skin cells dying in the wrinkles on my face,
And my blood corpuscles rustle in a bustling veiny tract,
And my muscle fibres shrieking as they're creaking to contract,
And my wiry neurones firing as they face the awful facts –
'Cause listening to science - there's not much to laugh about:
The certainty is scary, and I'd rather be in doubt,

'Cause I hear the tight indignity of artificially-fucked cattle,
And the drips of icecaps melting sound like cancer's last death rattle;
When I hold a shell up to my ear, I hear the noise of battle!
I'm enlightened by and frightened by these endless sounds of science.
Like a turgid physics lesson, that drones for hour on hour,
I hear sparks of destruction in every source of power
And boardroom conversations in drugs companies turn sour
The sugar-coated pills of pain relief;

And I long to return to my days of disbelief,
When I just took it all for granted, no need to care or fear;
But my naïve inner child's been raped by this oral inner ear
That sends unceasing to my brain the senseless sounds of science.

But there are far more important things for me to ponder on,
Like – have I set the Sky plus right? Will I get the ironing done?
And I'm fed up with listening to my metal molar shout;
So I've booked up with the dentist – gonna have the bugger out!
And tomorrow night when I'm in bed there'll be no auditory violence:
In the darkness I'll hear nothing but the sounds of silence.

My masculine side

Me, I'm in touch with my masculine side;
I still wash up, but badly,
Forgetting the roasting tin, leaving a tide
Of scum and grease and peas sadly
Stranded half-way up the sink.
For I am in touch with my masculine side,
And a disregard for mere hygiene, I think,
Is becoming; I take a certain pride
In the dirt round my neck, and the stink
From my armpits; you wouldn't catch
Me with deodorant – rarely even soap;
For I am in touch with my masculine side,
And you can't expect me to cope
With the children for more than one afternoon,
And that gives me a pass to spend noon
Until four on Sunday at the Slug and Bucket,
And when you complain I can say *Fuck it,*
Don't I deserve some time off, now and then?
And, sulking, go to my shed, and hide;
But I am in touch with my masculine side,
Which means that, just now and again
I want to be on top; I want to drive
You like I drive the car, certain that I am best
At each of these skills; I need you to connive
With me in this fantasy, for still inside
I am a little child scared of failing a test;
Yes, I am in touch with my masculine side.
And if, for one moment, you thought that I cried
When last year my father suddenly died,
You'd be wrong; I kept it all shut up inside,

But I'm really in touch with my masculine side,
And I need to conquer the world.
I need to kill wolves, bring back food to the cave;
I'll never be another man's slave;
I want to triumph, see my flag unfurled;
I want to be leader, to be needed as guide,
For I am in touch with my masculine side,
And a man wouldn't keep this within -
Sometimes I just want to win!

Miaow

Here's a feathered present; just a trifle
I caught for you outside. Not that I get any thanks -
You'd think birds grew on trees. You vegetarian cranks
Just don't see things like I do -
Your response, at best, is to stifle
A scream, and screw
Up your nerves to pick up the bird and throw it in the bin.

Ok, so feed me then. Whatever's in the tin
Today, I'll turn my nose up, yawn,
Inspect my paws - and eat it when you've gone.

Me, a pet? Get real -
I do just what I feel.
And if that happens to include
Lying on my back and stretching, lewd
And unashamed, with every little whisker twitch
Enticing you to scratch my itch,
Inviting you to stroke my ears and rub my head, to
Tickle hard that bit on my neck, just there,
And - oh, don't stop, please, no not there, yes *there,*
Oh that's it, more more more please more -
No, my head, you fool, forget my paw -
Oh yes, oh yes, Oh God of cats now now now now
Prrr prrr prrrr prrrr prrrrr prrrrr
Miaow.....

Fall from Grace

In January, I fell from Grace -
Which is the name I give my ladder now.
I thought I could rely on her -
Together we'd rise higher and higher -
But I was wrong. The capricious cow
Turned into a two-faced liar
And slipped, *accidentally* - like the lovers who desert you
And swear they never meant to hurt you -
On mossy paving stones;
Pulled the rung out from under my feet,
And dumped me, none too gently;
And as we parted, left me not broken-hearted
But with a shattered heel bone.
The smooth promontory of my calcaneum
Had become an archipelago,
Or so the X-ray seemed to show:
With clear black channels between each chalky isle.
This will take a while to mend, they said,
As I lay on the hospital bed.
Six weeks in plaster, six in a contraption,
And then you'll have to learn to walk again.
Which I must say was a damper, and put an end to the poet's rapture
I had felt when I found that this is called a lover's fracture,
Traditionally sustained by people leaping from high windows
            to avoid capture
By their paramours' husbands or wives -
They'd rather risk their lives than be caught in the act.
And I'd like to claim this as my story, but it is a disappointing fact
That I missed out on the good bits and the glory.
I just fell.
I had torn ligaments as well,
And I suffered mild concussion, too; confused, I'd do things
            I'd already done.
And I suffered mild concussion, too; confused, I'd do things
            I'd already done.
But the worst bump of my tumbling percussion
Thumped my bum,

92

Which, after my poor foot struck stone,
Landed on the ladder,
Which was by now prone (or possibly supine - it's hard to tell with ladders)
So that between aluminium and pelvic bone was crushed muscle -
Which is not as you might think a Swedish heavy metal band,
Or a belittled bivalve,
Or something dished up by Heston Blumenthal.
My blooming fall left me unable to sit or lie or stand
Without a very literal pain in the arse.
And it will take months or even years to pass.

And yes, I know it could have been much worse -
I don't need you or any nurse to tell me that.
And at least I've now a vague idea
Of what it's like to wake each morning with the fear
Of aches that stretch to the horizon,
Punctuated by telegraph poles of immobility.
Though I've had just a few short weeks of trivial disability,
I won't forget what I have learned.
But my mind was full of my own concerns when a friend said,
Hasn't it made you grateful that you're usually so fit?
No! Not a bit.
Never mind the inconvenience and pain -
I am not the same.
I always hated it when people said *Take care.*
I'd started a campaign to say instead, *Take risks!*
I never turned a hair at danger;
I got my kicks jumping out of aeroplanes;
I was someone who dared.
But now I think I'm scared.
Perhaps that fearless woman I once was just isn't there any more.

It's hard to pick up courage when you've been dumped in the dirt,
But I want to be what I was before,
And though I'll never touch Grace again, the treacherous little flirt,
I know I must find another ladder, and climb like I've never been hurt.

Goodnight
She hears the key turn in the back door lock.
Her hand goes to her head, she sighs and stands,
Goes into the kitchen. As usual, he isn't really drunk,
But far enough from sober. He asks her for a beer;
She pours him one, he drinks, belches, wipes his mouth,
Kisses her; then harder, noisy. *Ssh, the kids will hear,*
She says, but that won't stop him; it never has before.
He is dirty, and he smells; smoke and filth and sweat;
She turns her face away. A button hits the floor.
His hand pulls inside her bra, freeing her left breast;
He kneads it like a lump of dough,
Then sinks his teeth in hard, twice, three times. *I know*
"You like that, don't you? he says, and his face wears
An awful smile. He chews her more,
 Don't, she says, but he just looks at her and swears,
His fingers wrenching lower at her clothes,
Probing deep, intruding, and invading her. *Come on, you whore,*
I know what you want, he says. She's pushed
            against the breakfast bar,
Her head is banged, her shoulders jarred,
And he's inside her, shoving, careless, dry.
In magazines they get so wet they're dripping, he complains;
It feels as if he's ripping her apart,
But she says nothing - better let it be.
But still it just gets worse. *Respond, you fucking bitch*, he snarls,
You could at least pretend; you used to want me -
There must be someone else, you little tart,
Or else we'd be all right. He jams his angry hand against her jaw,
Forcing, turning, so she cannot breathe; she tries
To push him off. He grabs her wrist and twists
It up behind her back. *Say after me, I am a dirty whore.*
But this is just too much.
She turns to face him, laughs at him, out loud; his fist
On her cheekbone stops her mockery.
He knocks her to the floor,
And she lies silent, waiting for his final
Goodnight kick.

On falling in love with the wrong man
When a mountain climber trips,
And is hanging by his fingertips
Above an inescapably fatal fall,
Does he use his final breath
To shout out "No!" in the face of death,
Or "Yes!" with the exhilaration of it all?

Clownfish
If you were a fish, then the kind of fish you'd be
Is a brightly-coloured clownfish, the joker of the sea.
You'd titillate your audience, throwing buckets of fresh air,
And the bravest little sea-shrimps would touch you, for a dare.
You'd pratfall over flatfish, have mud pies waved in your face;
You'd get standing ovations, even from the plaice.
But when the show was over, and the shoal had had their thrills
They wouldn't see the sad, sad look, clinging to your gills,
For though he may seem happy, he's not how he appears –
The clown fish is always crying, but the kind sea hides his tears.

Dream seeds
And yet it all seemed right;
However bad things were before
I never dreamt of rescue by a knight
In shining armour;
I wanted a real man,
A fireman or a farmer,
With days of rain and rays
Drawn on his face,
With scars and silence, pain kept in its place,
And hardness built into his frame,
But still a boy, enjoying the same
Rough pleasures he had always loved,
And loving me in the untamed
Way of creatures we hear howling in the night.

And here he is;
A drinker and a thinker,
With muscles built from living use
And synapses like sinews;
A man who understands the trees,
A boy who knows how to seize
My soul, and bring back the girl
Who would have shared the seas
With dolphins;
A public poet and a painter of private rainbows,
A sower of dream-seeds, a man who chose
Me, for now, to receive his rhymes and words,
And made me want the freedom of the birds.

But freedom is for fighters,
And strong cages make good writers,
And dreams, like dreamers, always tell you lies;
And although – because – he cares,
He – we – cannot disguise
The truth; that he who dares
To harvest dreams, reaps always, only, nightmares.

First reactions

What do you do when you're told you are dying,
And it's fatal cancer that's made you so ill?
Do you go in for wailing and crying,
Ask which mad politician to kill?
Or do you postpone the blame and the sighing,
Like Pete, and say,
            "I wish I hadn't paid that bloody income tax bill!"

In the snow
In the snow there are dead things;
An orphaned foxcub, old squirrels,
A boar, bled to death after a fight.
You can feel them in the night;
Still whole, their souls refuse to leave,
Can't believe spring's light
Won't open eyes shut tight
Against the cold.

An earthy death bed is proper and right,
Makes us give back stuff we lend
And borrow; for some new creature's turn.
Every beginning is another beginning's end,
And free atoms have the chance to learn
Another shape;
　　　　　　　　But not like this,
Held, and useless,
Not to be awakened with a kiss,
Or allowed to burn
On a warrior's boat with set sails,
Drifting, or to return
To the water's dissolving bliss,
Absolved with a burial at sea.
The snow's hug fails
To finish what is started
With a conclusion;
Death and life cannot find fusion
Till the icy bonds are parted
By the sun;
And I need its warmth on me.

Losing your wings
Gentle angel, sunshine to my sleep,
Ripple to my deep
Waters, unfeathered wings unfurled to keep
Me safe; weep
No more. You came
From light; lift your face now to the same
Brightness you bring me. You shower yourself with shame
For things long gone, beat yourself black with blame;
But you have paid for
All of that; dark thoughts can fade or
Die now. You were made for
This final scene; the rest was just rehearsal
For the part you've played for
Me. Soon, there'll be rôle reversal.
You will not be alone;
Your nightmares will be known
To me, your demons turned to stone;
I will destroy despair,
Send sadness packing, stroke your hair
With soft breezes. I'll be there,
A smiling seraph, every morning when you wake;
But, angel, help me get there, take
My hand one last time; shake
Off your wings, for I'll need them to fly,
And angels who've been very good qualify
For humanity again. So, no angel, just my woman –
        this kiss won't be goodbye.

Dying men

Lovely ladies, lunatics and lords
Can get away with anything they please,
But there is another group who, justly so,
Is afforded the same privileges as these:

Dying men.
Dying men are entitled to be rude;
They can ask for meals, then turn their nose up at your food,
Or worse still eat it and throw up on the sofa.
They can use you without conscience, while they loaf a-
Round doing nothing all day long.
They'll tell you to your face that you are boring,
And keep you up all night with thunderous snoring,
Then expect you to amuse them when they wake.
A relationship to them means take and take;
For they are special people, held in almost Godlike awe.
They are getting off at life's next stop, they are no more
Of our kind; they are guests within humanity,
And we are obliged to offer them hospitality
Of all kinds; they are white elephants, a gift, a token
Of esteem, which we serve gladly, though we're broken
By the burden. So we hold precious each bitter minute of our care,
Fearing later knowledge of every deed undone, each rare
Moment lost. We forgive everything, and continue quietly crying;
They have us in their power, even without trying;
And we blame ourselves for everything, just because they're dying.

This poem is repetitive
This poem is repetitive,
But then show me an old song that isn't.
This poem is repetitive,
But if I go on enough you might listen

This poem is repetitive,
But then again, so is grass;
Over-engineering, they call it;
It means that it's built to last.

This poem is repetitive,
But so is blue sky above you,
And some things are meant to be said many times,
Like I'm sorry, and I love you.

This poem is repetitive,
But it moves with a purposeful beat,
For a poet measures his life between
The steps of his metric feet.

This poem is repetitive,
Just like my husband's snoring;
This poem is repetitive,
And it could get very boring,
Like the cancer pains in his back, and his chest,
That hit him again and again;
But knowing what the alternative is,
He's the most tolerant of men.

This poem is repetitive,
But so's God, he keeps making mistakes;
It's always good people who suffer,
It's always the wrong ones he takes
Away
So I'll say
It once more;
For I'm sure
That though this poem is repetitive,
Isn't life all repetition?

Awakenings, doubts, iniquities,
Hopes, disappointment, contrition;
And if what I say makes a difference,
I'll go on and on till I drop,
But poetry never changed anything,
So I'll stop.

Epithalamion

I, Brenda Mary, take thee, Peter Anthony,
To my lawful wedded husband,
To have and to hold,
Especially when it's cold,
But if holding is too painful,
I will understand
If our contact is restricted to
The touch of hand on hand;
In sickness and in sickness –
We don't envisage health,
And though there might be fame,
It's unlikely there'll be wealth;
There's a bitter irony about
Till death do us part,
But advantages in knowing
Where you're going from the start;
Then, for better – ah, for better
Is the essence here because
Since you found me, or I found you,
Whichever way it was,
A new dimension's added
To the life I had before –
You're a man who lets the world in,
You're a man who opens doors,
And it tickles me the way you
Want my promise to obey you,
But I feel cherished every day that you
Are near;
And, Pete – I'm glad we're here.

I know he hears

The man I love is broken, dying,
Uneasy fingers twitching at the sheets
In a chemical confusion, and I am lying by him
On a reclining chair, in undue mid-June heat,
Waiting for each breath, hearing the illusion of a sigh
From the inflated mattress, every time he moves.
The oscillating fan exhales in its incessant grooves,
And he says nothing, muttering, groaning
Sometimes, and the stuttering of the syringe driver
Punctuates his quiet.
                                But I know he hears;
For when I try to soothe his restless fumbling, calm his fears
By stroking him and mumbling *I love you*,
I sometimes add, *If you love me, squeeze my hand*;
And I feel his fingers tighten; we understand.

It's not like this in the movies

It's not like this in the movies;
The sheets are all snowy and clean,
And the hero looks pale in a cool sort of way,
Not haunted, grey, bone-lean.

It's not like this in the movies;
They don't cry with pain at each touch;
Brothers don't wait a day, they come straight away;
Real people don't care so much.

It's not like this in the movies;
They take delicate sips from a cup,
They don't vomit and retch for hours at a stretch,
You don't see the black bile they cough up.

It's not like this in the movies;
Lovers stay by the bed just one night;
They don't have to decide between the last bit of pride,
And just giving up on the fight.

It's not like this in the movies;
They just wipe away a brave tear.
They don't yell and howl as they throw in the towel,
But that's what it's like for us here.

It's not like this in the movies;
Happiness lies just round the bend;
There's a sweet final fold when the credits have rolled
But reality has no end.

Where are you now?
Oh Pete, where are you now?
I am drowning in the sounds of kindly words
From people calling, I am falling
Down a sympathetic well,
And I think that you are talking
But your voice just can't be heard
Above the splutters and the squawking
Of the comforters from hell.

And I know it's my fault really;
Quite clearly if I chatter on for ever
Then the clatter and the clamour
Will hammer in the memories,
Reinforce reminders, and the kindest people
Let me prattle on;
But part of me wants silence, craves for stillness,
Then perhaps I'll hear your voice as it was before your illness
Tamed it, damped it down, clamped around your lungs
And took your breath,
Till it was gone.

Pete, please, talk to me now. Your death
Has robbed me of my man, my friend,
My lover and my husband, my dream-seed sower,
My grower of ideas, my inspiration;
And if our communication is to end,
Then what point is there in life?
I just want to be your wife
Again, share the laughs, the tears, the crack;
Pete, please, come back.

It's time I changed the bed
The sweat-stained sheet is still there on our bed;
I can smell you on the pillow where once was your poor head,
Full of pain and plans and sorrow,
And I tell myself tomorrow
I will clear your stuff away;
But that's exactly what I promised yesterday.

Land of the dead
I don't know what
I don't know what
I don't know what I'm supposed to do here
I've never been here
I've never been here in the land of the dead
I've never been here in the land of the dead
Should I shake my head, shed a single tear
Should I soak the bed, should I just fuck instead?
I don't know what I'm supposed to do here.

Should I just do what I want?
Should I just do what I want?
Morphine freedom's what I want
I want that morphine freedom ride
I want to hide, I want to hide
Don't watch as I curl up and die inside
Don't watch as I curl up and die inside
And it's all still there by his side of the bed
Under the chair on his side of the bed
Bottles of morphine, bottles of dead
And they'd fix the pain in my heart and my head
Ten brown bottles, waiting to be clear
Ten brown bottles and they could be clear instead
And it wouldn't take that many to be sure that I was…

I don't know what I'm supposed to do here
I don't know what I'm supposed to do here
And I don't know how to get through here
In the land of the dead.

Requiem

Once this was a poet,
Who cast lines about his life to leave me reeling,
Then drew me in; danced me round and round
And left me feeling
Punch-drunk, intoxicated, slugged
With a thought I should always have known.
He quickened me; drugged
With shoals of words I was shown
Shy creatures hiding; I could grasp eels
And see through Catherine wheels
And have my skin turned outside in
Before he knocked my senses to the ground.

Once this was a man
Who lay beside me in the dark;
Who shared with me his spliffs
And his laughter in wild riffs
Of well-phrased fantasy,
And made me realise the stark
Uncompromising future there must be –
Things or thoughts; a choice that had been too hard for me.

Once this was my lover,
And our bed shared more than words;
And when your body too has heard
The silver singing of a man complete
As this, then sentences are mute,
Phrases flat, images, however sweet,
Stay grounded; his poetry, like his love, was total, absolute;
A language with syntax of sinew and a vocabulary wrapped
In skin; emotions never could stay trapped,
Unexpressed, for him.

Without a poem, a day is merely time;
Without this poet, life no longer has rhyme
Or season,
And there can be no God-given reason
For taking him away.
Once this was a poet;
But that was yesterday.

Counting seconds

Six hundred and four thousand and eight hundred blades of grass
Invite me to lie down,
Feel their freshness, count the seconds pass
In this field flowing with life, and on the ground
Where I stretch naked, crying,
Ten thousand and eighty insects bustle, trying
Hard to fill each minute, as he tried;
And one hundred and sixty-eight apple trees
Hold hands around me as they did when I slept by his side
Here, in this field, for what seemed endless hours.
Seven sheep baa through their peaceful days,
As they always did till evening,
And just as I begin to think of leaving,
I can see high in the haze
A solitary hawk gliding free, free-wheeling,
Watching over me; one week's gone by,
Now, since I saw my lover die.

Tidy

The CDs on the rack are in order;
No books now, are waiting unread;
For once, there's no weeds in the border;
Life is tidy, now you are dead;
But my mind is still full of litter, my head
Can't be cleared of the mess, the disorder,
The distraction, of all of the words left unsaid.

Tendernitis

When a broken bone mends, it ends up stronger than before,
While muscles, torn or strained, just heal weaker, fragile, small;
And we think that if you've had hard times, you get tougher,
        can take more –
But hearts are only muscle, after all.

Suicidal?
It says a lot about what the last eight years have been to me,
That I can say with expert knowledge, and absolute certainty –
The Samaritans just aren't what they used to be.

I will forget you
When the moon takes away a shiver
And the sun fills me with cold
And my feet do not deliver
Footprints to summer seas of gold;
When the lark sings loud at midnight
To the church bells' silent chime
And the hands of man clasp tight
Around the fingerslip of time;
When the tears are made of vinegar
And the morning sky is torn
And the ruffed unruffled singer
Wishes music wasn't born;
When the softness of the dying
Melts the ending of the year
When the words of love stop lying –
Then I will forget you, dear.

Swan

I never expected this.
When they said a sense of loss
I imagined emotions would be torn and tossed
Internally, perhaps eternally across the days
And nights of waking; making you stay near
Would merely mean replaying pictures,
Saying your words again and again
Until the tape wore thin.
But
I miss you with my skin,
My guts; nerve endings
Damaged, needing mending,
Fingers as well as hopes forlorn, I mourn
You with my muscles and my bone;
I understand so well the widowed swan who swims alone.
For this is animal; the brutality
Lies in the physicality; the tangible reality
Of isolation slices limbs off life,
And when parts are missing there can be no re-creation
Of totality, or of sense.
Certainty can only ever be in the past tense,
And nothing was as known as this last nothing;
No touch of love more felt than this
Endless embrace of your absence,
And death's final insubstantial kiss.

The last song

This shall be the last song I will write for you
        The moon is crying, and shines shy behind closed clouds
Already I am losing sight of you, your face
        Full of pain and kindness and sorrow
Does not look back from every mirror, every place
        Marked out by scars
Is not some where we went, or where we would have gone
        Shadowed by light not owned but borrowed
The sun that shone for us shines still
        And every night it gives a promise
        And I will not forget you
        All debts and doubts will be repaid
        I will not let you leave me; yet you
True as snow and sure as sterling
        Are fading from the world outside; but
The silver shiver given by the moon always remains;
        No bright day or dismal night can hide
The burn of ice, the vision that explains
        Love's pale recurring flame
The reason why unreason feels no shame
        I will have no fear of darkness now I know
        That life in all ways does not end with death
        Your silent light is in my every breath
        And every ending is a lie
        And as long as I will live, you shall not die.

I am a happy man
Cheltenham is full of flowers,
Line-dancing, promiscuous, in beds in the park,
Shaking in cages pinned to walls,
Nightclub performers left out after dark.
But there is a place where they are still;
A place you wouldn't know, perhaps,
Where you can wheel your husband, broken, ill
And dying, from his monitored bed,
To sit in aching sunshine for a while;
Where seeds have been sown,
And shrubs and benches planted
In memory of people now unknown.
In the hospital garden we sat each day,
Until even this tiny trip from technology
To biology became too far.
We watched June flowers learning to be tarts,
Thrusting forward their sexiest parts,
And, poet as he was,
It tickled him that burgeon rhymed with surgeon.
And I picked lavender for him; its sweet smell hit our hearts
And touched off scented tears, caught in our breath.
He sat there, crushed purple in his hand,
Not quite omnipotent emperor of his last few grains of sand,
And, four days away from death,
He said, *I am a happy man.*

Young offenders
The real test,
When I built a self-assembly chest
The other day,
Was to find a proper use
For the leftover nuts and screws,
And not just, puzzled, throw them all away.

Off and on
Pissed off, missed off, cut off, shut off, switched off,
Off, *off*, ***off***, **OFF**, ***OFF***!
Off cuts; offside; offlined; offhand,
Off heart.
Can art
Change this?
Creativity's kiss
Bring life to these unpowered sparks,
Illuminate the dark,
Reboot their systems, turn them all back on?
They are too young for energy to have gone,
But the circuit's disconnected;
Maintenance neglected,
And our message is rejected, spurned,
Returned unread to sender,
As if the 'end' in young offender
Is terminal. Dead.

Yes. They're pissed off, missed off, cut off, shut off;
They're switched off, ɛ ll right.
For them art's just a joke;
They'd rather have a smoke,
And all we can do is offer them
A light.

Like you
If I saw nothing in the clouds,
And fields and trees were only green;
If I sought comfort in sad crowds,
And thought the streets were dark and mean;

If love had never come my way,
And I'd learned nothing from my schools,
And every day was just a day,
And thrills came just from breaking rules;

If the sun gave me no pleasure;
Horizons always came out grey;
Rainbows meant no buried treasure,
And people were just lumps of clay;

If I had never lazed by streams
And pondered things that I could do;
If I did not believe that dreams
Had just a chance of coming true –

Then I might be like you,
I guess; I think I'd be like you.

And thieving cash to pay for spliffs
And spraying paint and smashing glass –
Forget about the buts and ifs –
Would be the best scenes in this farce;

Fun would come from masturbation,
Smirking sex and sniffing glue;
Without the rough joy of creation,
What else would I do?

Yes, I might be like you,
I guess; I would be like you.

Except me
I'm twelve years old.
In a prison cell, cold, grey,
Here all day and all last night.
Can't turn the light
On or off,
Or the eyes that watch,
Lobbing laughs, robbing privacy, rude;
And they've been gobbing in my food.
Metal bed; I stay awake.
Metal bog; no seat, no lid,
Nothing to smash or rip or break,
Or take;
Nothing to damage,
Except me.

Don't
Don't know
Don't care
Don't want
Don't feel
Don't think
Don't understand

Don't risk
Don't try
Don't fail
Don't wonder why
Don't talk
Don't cry

Don't make;
Break
Don't give;
Take

Don't
   live.

Cell
Cell
in a beehive
full of honey
full of buzzing
with a tiny larva
struggling, fussing,
trying to come alive.

Cell
in a weed
full of chlorophyll
and sunshine,
oozing sap; still
and snoozing,
and sheltering a seed.

Cell
in a body
with a purpose
and a function;
in the stream
of double helixes
working out a dream.

Cell.
In a prison.
Doors.
Locked.
Shut.

The same snow

The same snow shrouds the souls
Of those who trudge, force-footed, to the poles
Or toehold to the highest peaks;
The same snow, sheer, unseen, seeks
To erase emotion, cover love, clean
Over feelings with a fleece,
Till action seems the one release;
Violence a triumph over silence;
And bold endeavour or cold crime
Are sold to the psychology
As ways of overcoming time's
Enfolding tedium;
Extremes become the medium
Of expression –
A solitary self-defining obsession.

Perhaps it's all due to biology.
Sufferers of sluggish physiology
Need more stimulation, irritation
Than those of us who are content.
They are not crazy, wild or bent,
These men who have offended or explored;
With hearts, minds, bodies all born bored,
These ways are not what they have chosen –
Their paths lead to escape from being frozen.

Victims

A stolen car, a broken door;
Life's windows smeared by dirty fingers:
The stink of violation lingers
Long after reparation or replacement –
A body buried in the basement
Of the mind.

The perpetrators of these crimes
Have suffered from no theft
Defined by law;
But their existence
Is as empty as a plundered jewellery drawer;
No glow of beauty left,
No hope. Their loss is not insured;
Must be endured, time and again.

Who are the victims, then?

Gloucester prison

Anonymous as an anthill,
Repellent as Teflon,
This hiding place for human treasures
Threatens intruders,
Jangles keys all through the night,
Treads heavy along sad corridors,
Keeps a jealous watch on all within.
It hugs its inmates close and crowded
In its frozen heart, beating time;
A metronome of chaos,
A factory of fear.
It surely loves the ones it holds,
For it hates to let them go.

Prison education admin office

It could be anywhere.
Buttermilk-painted brick;
A ceiling tiled and flecked,
And stained where rain comes in;
Box folders racked on bracketed shelves,
And a calendar, with pictures of fast cars,
Dates ticked; the peck and click of keyboards.
But behind the window blinds
       are bars.

Three teabags and a plastic soldier

I've lived a life of crime and don't you doubt it.
Listen to this rhyme and I'll tell you all about it.
I'm big and I'm bad and there's no-one bolder -
Three teabags and a plastic soldier.

It started in Woolworth's, a shop like no other
I was seven years old. I was there with my brother.
He said *You're in trouble if you don't do what I say -*
See that toy soldier there, in the open tray?
He's coming home with us and you're going to take him.
Stuff him in your pocket and don't you bloody break him.
They won't suspect nothing - you're too little and sweet,
But let me down, sister, and you're dead meat.

I looked at the soldier and he aimed his gun at me.
I wasn't having that! With a sting like a bee
And the stealth of an assassin, I slipped him in my fist.
Nobody was looking and the soldier wasn't missed.
I was cool as any penguin as I strolled to the street.
Masterthief, me - it felt kinda neat,
But I was a professional and wouldn't push my luck,
So thumbs up to my bro and we ran like hell.

It was robbery with violence, but I didn't care.
I knew it was wrong but I didn't turn a hair.
I felt smarter than my bruv and ten years older -
And that's how it began, with a plastic soldier.

But in the dark of the night I cried at what I'd done,
And I hid away the soldier with his plastic gun.
I didn't want no evidence when coppers came to find me,
And I swore I'd never steal again - I put all that behind me.

Fifty years later, in a doctors' surgery;
A bunch of people waiting, and waiting for me.
They were my little writing group and it was time for tea,
And I'd run out of the pyramids - short by three.
The pressure was worse than the threats from my bro.
I swallowed back my conscience; I knew where to go.
In the cupboard in the corner was the doctors' secret store -
I was masterthief again as I opened up the door.

And with the courage of a leader who knows what has to be
I nicked those teabags, one, two, three,
Well, they had a hundred more, and I left a little letter.
Next week I put six back, so they ended up better.
And that's all I have stolen, in all my sixty years,
But - it's all been on my conscience, this criminal career
And I'm glad I've confessed; I'm relieved that I've told yer
Of the three teabags and a plastic soldier.

Haiku written in prison
Sunflower petals;
corn spirals; the same pattern –
God? Mathematics?

If I look at you
too much, you'll dazzle my eyes.
I need an eclipse.

Squirrels steal my nuts.
I don't begrudge them this, but –
they could leave me one.

Not Reading

I'm going to tell you a story about a prisoner, a con.
Of course, I can't give you his real name; for now, I'll call him Ron.
And I don't think at this moment I'll tell you about his crime –
It might prejudice your thoughts, though it never affected mine,
Because in my little writing group were an arsonist, a burglar,
Two rapists and a dealer, and, on my right, a murderer.
Three of them were given to bouts of real self-harm,
With aerial views of railway junctions blazoned on their arms.
AndtTheir lives were born of chaos. Most had been in what we call care,
Though I gathered from what they told me that there was only
       tough love there.
Ron's mum was paranoid, schizophrenic, and since he was a lad
He'd cared for her; it was all he knew; he didn't have a dad.
And he became agoraphobic; couldn't bear to go outside;
Started drinking. Within himself he slowly found a place to hide.
So for Ron you might think a prison cell was not such a bad place to be,
But, just like every prisoner, he wanted to be free,
And he found liberty in writing – poetry gave him wings.
He found his words; he found himself; he found a new song to sing.
I encouraged the group to think of things outside the prison walls.
Poetry's better than drugs, they said; and I guess that says it all.
It was a kind of therapy. In Ron's imagination
It was me that made him feel better. In truth, the joys of creation
Were what lifted him. But he got it wrong. He would never say
What was on his mind and in his heart, but a poem gave him away.
I've fallen in love with you, it was called. It was meant for me,
       that was clear,
And it explained why, when given a parole date, Ron's eyes
       had filled with tears.

Now, I've always thought that honesty's best. We sat down.
       I meant to explain.
But what I said was: *The imagery's weak. The rhythm's not right.*
       You'll need to work on it again.
Next week, Ron was nowhere to be found. I didn't understand,
Till I asked another guy from the group. He just stared down
       at his hands,
And said, *Didn't nobody tell you, miss? Ron jumped, from the*
       roof to the floor.
Nobody knows why he done it, miss, but 'e won't be round 'ere no more.

We all dragged out our mattresses; thought we might, like, break 'is fall,
But it's too far from up there and 'e's broken 'is back. We couldn't do
nothin' at all.

So, why did he do it? I'll never know. I'll never see Ron again.
The prison system's suspicious of anyone who dares call a con a friend.
Maybe the agoraphobia had launched his jump, his fall,
For the ultimate womb of death is surely the safest place of all.
I don't want to think my cold words were to blame; that's not how I
meant it to be;
And, perhaps, thinking in metaphors made him believe it was
the only way to be free.
But Ron was a man who could have known life, a person, just like
you and me,
And what I'm struggling to try and say, what I could have said
at the start,
Is that inside every prisoner – and I mean *every* prisoner –
Inside every one of us there beats a poet's heart.

ADHD

He's got ADHD, and he won't keep still.
He's got ADHD, and I swear I'm going to kill him.
He's got ADHD, and he tells me that he's ill,
But I believe that he's just fidgety,
As pernickety as pepper in your eyes,
And at the moment I despise him
For inventing this disease
As a torment and a tease,
Aimed at me and all the others,
Who he thinks of as his brothers...
They are slumped and staring down,
While he is pacing round and round,
And they are thinking, just like me,
Why the fuck won't he sit down?
But being the good teacher that I am,
I pretend that I don't give a damn,
And allow myself just the faintest frown.

Later he explains:
He's only just been diagnosed,
And now at last he knows
Why he did the things he did
When he was just a scruffy kid;
That brought his foster parents tears
And a sentence of eight years when he was older -
Arson.
The living room carpet. Lots of cars, and a forest,
And a café full of people. No-one died.
He explains
That he had itching powder in his veins;
That he always felt the rats that were rasping in his guts,
And the heavy metal songs that were sawing in his lungs,
And a hornet clashed and clattered like a train
In his brain, and he was wired,
He explains; he was so tired.
And the flames and the fire
Were the only things that soothed him;
The burning smoothed the burrs and the
Rawness of his skin,
And he could only be happy with a lighter in his hand.
And he said,
Do you understand, miss? Do you understand?

And I thought back. I thought back
To double physics,
When time passed with the speed of lichen;
When the sickness of boredom was as real
As gastric flu; when I too could feel
The rats, and the hornets; the mad songs;
And the morning stretched as long
As the forest he had lit up as a boy.

But I didn't set fire to the carpet,
Or the cupboards, or Katie the class swot,
Or even Mr. Carpenter, the physics teacher,
Despite the Bunsen burners tempting on each bench.

I didn't blaze.
I had the extinguisher of education,
The hose of hope.
I had the tools to cope.
I had all the luck.
Although inside there was a glow,
A slow smouldering, I came to know,
As words; as poetry.
And, some time later, so did he.
Eventually he dumped the drugs
That roped the rats and held the hornets;
Softened the songs to silence.
He learned to write, and didn't need the violence
Of a flame. He came to me one day and said,
I've still got the lighter, miss, but now it's in my head,
And in the pen that's in my hand.
Do you understand, miss, do you understand?
That I had ADHD, and I was ill;
But with words I've found the way, the will
To spit my sparks and light the dark,
Leap higher, dance with fire, and yet be still?

I allowed myself the faintest smile,
And left him working there,
Because at last the little sod was writing,
Sat down in a chair.

This man is innocent

You're in a hotel; it's the end of a long day.
An hour in the bar will take the stress away.
You see a pretty woman, sitting on her own.
She looks kinda nice. Why should you be alone?
So you offer her a drink. She accepts, with a smile -
She's pleased to have company. You chat for a while.
She's split up with her husband, and it's left her feeling low.
Your divorce has been horrific. She seems to want to know,
And before you are aware of it, the midnight hour has struck.
She kisses you goodnight. Perhaps you are in luck.
She says she has enjoyed herself; she's glad she caught your eye,
And she tells you her room number. Leaves you wondering why.

You finish off your whisky, have a pee, and sit and think.
Twenty minutes pass. Maybe you'll have another drink -
But you're longing for the comfort found within a woman's arms.
You're both adults, unattached - what could be the harm?
And - giving you her number? That was a hint, for sure.
And just five minutes later you are knocking at her door.
She sees you through the spyhole, unlocks and lets you in,
And now it's sheer desire that is burning up your skin,
And you take her by the hand and you lead her to the bed,
And you kiss her and caress her - but what has she just said?
I'm not sure that I want to.
                               Please - just for tonight.
What could be a problem? Everything will be all right.
And she is tugging at your zip and you're fumbling with her bra,
And you know it's going to happen, now you have got this far...
And, oh, it feels so good to be inside a woman again,
And you do your best to make it good for her as well, but then
She says *No, please. I'm sorry. Somehow it all feels wrong.*
And you stop what you are doing, and curse. After so long
To be pushed away again - it's almost more than you can bear,
But you dress yourself, apologise, and leave her lying there.

And soon it's all forgotten; it was just one of those things.
Till one day, two months later, you hear the doorbell ring
And two policemen ask you questions. You've been accused of rape,
And it's your word against hers. It seems there's no escape

123

Still, you know you are not guilty, so the trial holds no fear,
But your lawyers let you down, and you're sentenced to - five years!
Five years for feeling lonely, taking up an invitation?
Five years for being normal? This was no aberration.

As a woman, I resent this. Rape is never right,
But, you know, two people were inbolved in what went on that night.
To say that she was pressurised is not true; it's demeaning
To all women; robs equality of meaning.
If regret were a crime then we all would be inside.
She made a mistake.
                                        And then she lied,
Who knows with what reason, or what was her intent,
But I am in no doubt that this man is innocent.

First visit
Two forms of id, with address,
Closed in her bag,
And in her hand, two train tickets.
There's a queue; wives and girlfriends, mostly.
WAGs, she thinks, and tries a shuttered smile.
It doesn't really work.
Is this where Daddy works now? asks her son,
With far more questions in his open face.
Her phone is captured in a locker.
They wait inside a glass box, an aquarium;
Light and stares flow in,
And when a uniform with double keys arrives,
They all flood out, past dogs
With wagging tails and wary noses,
Through clanging gates and doors painted the blue
That she remembers from Ibiza.
Even the chairs cannot escape;
Bolted to the floor.
She feels like bolting,
But slams her best smile on,
Gives her son her hand to cling to,
And opens her mouth to speak -
Only to find that she has been shut up.

Where edges meet
I don't want to be part of you -
Your separateness delights me;
The unbridged gap between our skins
Entices and invites me.

I don't want to be apart from you -
Our closeness warms, enfolds me;
The soft friction where the edges meet
Is what, so firmly, holds me.

Beggars
Can you spare some coins for a cup of tea?
He was young, with a lurcher on a lead;
Not the sort to get sympathy from me,
Or handouts.
But still, I gave, as if doubts
About existence
Could be bought off with pence.
Yet which of us had greater need?

Because the small change of affection,
Cast carelessly in my direction,
Is what I ask of you, each time I call,
My hangdog phone seeking scraps.
That young man and I – we are a pair, perhaps,
For love makes beggars of us all.

If I were...

If I were a man, then any time
I could write an ode to the beauty of your body;
I could say that the hairs on your chest,
when you rise from our bed,
remind me of dawn ferns unfurling,
and have an otter's sleekness,
when you are in water.

If I were a sculptor, working in spring,
I could go further,
remark that your ribs
are spaced specially to fit my fingers;
and that your legs have the solid curves
of a tree; not young, whippy, impermanent,
and not yet old, scarred and brittle,
but moving, flexible; rooted.

If I were in a summer garden,
I could find vegetable comparisons
for the firmness of your buttocks to my touch –
onions, perhaps, canteloupes, probably,
and I would liken your laugh
to one of many sounds of nature.

I probably wouldn't say much about your feet,
but if I were an artist in the autumn light,
I could outline your ears,
trace your collarbones,
crosshatch your bearded cheeks;
comment on the contrast between our bodies,
seen together in a mirror –
your thunder and my rain.

But I am none of these, and this is winter;
nature is unfriendly, days are short;
and I can speak only of
the early fall of dusk on your tired eyes,
and touch you as you sleep, before I say goodbye..

NCP

Strip lights and concrete.
The sign said NCP.
The end of our first date,
And this near-stranger looked at me

And the strip lights became candles,
And the concrete wasn't bare
But hung with rainbow velvet.
The watchman wasn't there,
And the ticket machine was humming
A new and lovely tune,
And he kissed me. And the strip lights
Turned into a full moon
And the winter chill of concrete
Held the sunshine of the spring,
And the echo of cars leaving
Was a choir about to sing.
The exhaust fumes smelt like perfume,
And the strip lights burned inside me,
And this stranger was the lover
Who I hoped would stay beside me
All my life...

We arranged to meet next day.
He smiled, and walked away.

And the strip lights were just glaring,
And the concrete dull and bare,
But I knew this was the real thing,
And my feelings quite proportionate,
When I found I didn't care
That this *was* NCP,
And the charges were extortionate.
It cost me a small fortune, parking for our date,
But £10-50 for new love? That's not a bad rate.

Rainbows

You are
A rainbow resting on a wet black road;
The long muscles in my back when I've dumped a heavy load;
The unseen solution to a secret code;
A much better subject for an ode
Than a Grecian urn.

You are
The fractal pattern of the finest fern;
The smell of a pine tree beginning to burn;
Worth more money than I could ever earn;
The adrenaline rush when it's my turn
To perform.

You are
The flashes of lightning in a summer thunderstorm;
The very last box on the tax return form;
The furthest there could ever be from the norm;
The best way I know of getting warm
In bed.

You are
My A to Z, my daily bread,
The clearest thoughts that fill my head,
The greatest books I've ever read,
The gold that doesn't come from lead,
The second skin I'll never shed;
How I'd really like to spend my time instead
Of writing poems about rainbows.

Boulder

On my shoulders
I carry a boulder:
My love;
But each ice-pick remark,
Every chiselled comment chips it,
Scores a blaze,
A mark,
Unweathered, raw;
Dislodges a sharp splinter,
Or a sullen lump of flint, and
So the passing painful days
Leave it smaller than before;
Till finally it will fall away,
When a shrug, dismissive, tips it
To the floor,
Just a pebble now,
Unnoticed,
Not a burden any more.
And I am freed from all love's trouble,
With nothing more to show
Than a little pile of rubble –
The grave cairn of a love
I used to know.

Betrayed

Last night, my love, I slept with you; tonight I am with him
To whom I'm tied. Soon he will wake,
And gracelessly expect to take
His pleasures, his rights. His every whim
I will submit to; I will fake
Responses; tacitly allow him to invade
Our territory, once more stake
His alien claim to private places where we stayed;
To have possession of the gentle dreams we made.

Yet the world thinks he's the one who is betrayed.

Back

There was a time I loved him, this is true,
And sorting through his clothes has brought it back,
Though long before he died I had met you –
I pray that you don't have a heart attack.

The power of his charm took me aback;
It hit me like a heavyweight's one-two.
It wasn't a romance - more like a smack;
There was a time I loved him, this is true.

He died quite young, as I thought he might do.
His lifestyle meant his body took some flak –
A body which that other woman knew;
And sorting through his clothes has brought it back.

Love died before he did; he left the track,
Derailed by her small bum and eyes of blue,
But, as in rhyme, Jill's better off than Jack,
And long before he died, I had met you.

But now I worry – what else can I do?
Although of willing men there seems no lack,
I couldn't bear it if I lost you too –
I pray that you don't have a heart attack.

So every night when we have hit the sack,
Please share with me a sexual act or two.
This active fun will stop you getting slack,
And make sure that you live past fifty-two.
There was a time I loved him...

Don't go out tonight

Don't go out tonight.
The moon is full,
Turning milk sour,
And flirtations into serious affairs.

Don't go out tonight.
The stars shine brightly,
Hoping to be compared to candles,
And the light in a lover's eye.

Don't go out tonight.
The wind is high,
Lifting skirts and spirits,
And casting a blow for freedom.

Don't go out tonight.
The nightingale is singing,
And although we're miles from any square in London,
He still brings magic to the air.

Don't go out tonight.
The street lights glow in the dark
Like amber fires,
Sodium-lit stepping stones leading you away.

Don't go out tonight.
The highwaymen are out,
Stealing money, jewels and valuables,
And possibly your heart.

Don't go out tonight.
The house is cold and empty when you've gone,
And I am numb with a hollow feeling
That you might never fill it up again.

Gone now

Gone now;
Not a bit like dew wiped dry by the sun,
Or stars faded by daylight,
Or roses browned off by the autumn,
Or sandcastles smashed by the sea;
Who gives a damn about them?
Their going leaves only memories with smiles attached,
And anyway, they'll be back,
At the next dawn or dusk, spring or summer;

But you are gone now,
And it's more like
A multiple motorway pile-up,
Whole towns smothered by landslides,
Countries devastated by freak floods.
This is serious business,
And I won't compare it with pretty things -
It is more violent, a matter of more impact,
And the force of it jolts all breath from me,
Dislodges happiness from memories,
Removes feeling from sense.
You are gone now;
You won't be back,
And I won't diminish that
By talk of stars and roses.

Socks

For some men, bits of clothing are a necessary spice
In the recipe for making love; there's nothing can entice
Them like a wisp of nylon stocking, and a glimpse of a suspender
Belt, with firm white thigh between them - they need these to engender
The desire required for action, the incentive to perform
In the bed, or on the sofa; just to keep their ardour warm
There must be satin, silk or lace upon the female skin -

But not my man; he likes me in the outfit I came in
When I was born, from head to knees; naked, nude, quite bare,
No make-up and no jewellery, no sexy underwear.

132

My mind's freed from discomfort - for suspenders, to be sure,
Are the most irritating garment that a human ever wore -
So, released from this encumbrance, I give total concentration
To providing waves of physical, full-contact stimulation.
But still, we all have foibles, and to keep his passion sweet
I must wear these white fluffy things; although quite clean, my feet
Alone do nothing for him; yes, the soft key that unlocks
My funny lover's lusty interest in sex, is socks.

Car park

There are spaces in the car park;
Clumped at the far end,
Dotted near the office
Window, where I stand looking
At the one space, light and dry,
Where all around is dark
From recent rain, the space
Where your car was, until
A moment past, when
With a wave, you turned,
And drove away, leaving
A dry, blank, empty space
In the car park, which I
Stare at now, eyes dry,
With no tears yet, numb
And empty, with a gap
In my life, like the space
Where your car was, until
A moment past.

Tonight

She's got him tonight.
She'll smile at him as he walks through the door,
Look flirtatious, dimming down the light,
Just a little, handing him a Scotch,
Just how he likes it. Lovingly she'll watch
As he eats the meal she's carefully prepared,
And with a leaden simper, when he asks for more,
Say, "I thought we could have dessert upstairs."

He'll follow meekly; he would never dare
Disturb the peace, despite the war
In his emotions, and in mine.

She's naked now, in fleshy splendour standing there before
Him; it's not for him, he knows; she's staking a claim
To the physical, because she cannot own his mind.

So it continues to its bitter end; doing the same
Things that we do, a gruesome pantomime
Which I can feel, a hundred miles away;
Skins sticking, tongues tangling, hands clammy with the touch
Of places where he touched me only yesterday.
And he believes we can cut off that place, that time
From this - but no, their bodies writhe together
Like monsters in my head, inescapable, whether
I close my eyes or open them, I always know.

But it's not them; what brings about such
Damage to my soul is all my own -
Oh God, I wish this stupid fucking jealousy would go.

First kiss

A field made gold
By sunshine and by buttercups;
A February bus stop
On the main A41,
With wind-blown strands of hair
Between our lips;
An unexpected New Year midnight moment,
In someone else's bright two-up, two-down;
The touch of little finger upon finger
On a polished desk, in
An office full of strangers
Who knew nothing;
A hotel room; a hotel room;
A hotel room; an orchard
Where the apples seemed to ripen
As we stood, bewildered, at a
Deadly open gate; Manchester airport,
Terminal number two - this time
An August bus stop;
And a car park, where the concrete
Turned to velvet, for my very last
First kiss.

Reciprocity

There is no reciprocity in life, my lover said.
Men love women, women love children, and children love hamsters,
And hamsters only love to shred
Old love letters to make a bed.

If you wish to part
If you wish to part,
Then will you quietly leave
In early morning dark,
Slipping through a sleeve
Of shadow to your clear-sighted light;
Drop no word to ripple my pool
Of sleep; allow the night
To darken still the vision of the fool
You leave behind;
Will you place a note for me to find
Which, when unfolded, opens up my eyes
And stamps ink-sharp upon my mind
The truth, or, better still, the final lies?

Or will you handle me like tangled string,
Neatly tie off all the ends,
Patiently go through everything
That's wrong between us, say we'll still be friends
Now that we've got it straight;
Explaining all, except the reason why,
Because you say it's just too late
For that; that it is time to say goodbye;

Or will you carefully arrange a fight,
A verbal boxing match within a ring
Which you create, never quite
Landing a merciful knockout blow, bringing
Me back from the oblivion where care has died,
Each time, with words that count out
The ways that we have loved, while you hide
Behind a guard of seeming doubt;

Or will it be like it is now -
Finding each other less and less,
Wondering just why and how;
Then fading into nothingness?

My dog misses you

It's my dog that misses you, not me -
The casual hand that gently stroked his head,
The one who tidied blankets for his bed -
My dog misses you, not me.

My dog misses you, not me -
The times when you joined in his silly games,
The way you used to call him soppy names;
The silent physical joy of being near,
Silently absent now that you're not here;
My dog misses you, not me.

My dog misses you, not me.
His senses tell him better than mine do -
For him there is a tangible lack of you;
There is an essence missing, one smell less
Around the house, and that the sweetest and the best,
The liveliest, most full of interest,
Warm and rich and deep; love, so wordlessly expressed.
Hell was once described as an endless sense of loss.
Well, that's where my dog is now - it's as if he's passed across
From this world's joys. He just sits, depressed,
And so do I, to keep him company.
It's my dog that misses you, not me.

Tongues first

Tongues first; before our lips meet, fluids mingle;
No paddling in shallows here, no ginger steps on shingle,
But a dive into the mouth's sweet oyster.
When tongues tangle, there's a tingle
Of immediate desire, a foretaste of the moister,
Deeper places, and a knowledge of the body's knots
To follow – coupled limbs, doubled skins, loops and slots
Threaded through with pleasure. Yes; when bold tongues call the shots,
What pair of able bodies can stay single?

How long

How long does it take?
How long does it take –
  for lightning to strike?
  to learn to ride a bike?
  to cross a road?
  to crack a code?
  to find a prince inside a toad?
  for a candle to burn?
  for a fool to learn?
  to change your mind?
  to switch from lined paper to freeform?
  for coldness to become warm?
  to make a man cry?
  for an old love to die?

  to write another verse?
  to throw away a purse (well, who needs money)?
  to see why a joke is funny
  but this is serious stuff?
  to know when it's time enough
  to say I love you?
  to fall asleep with the falling light?
  to want to be wrapped in you instead of sheets at night?
  to affect the meaning of everything I write?
  to go from conversation to a kiss?
  to tell you that tonight, my love, I miss you?

Like Everest, really

I'm trying to tell you things I couldn't say,
And if I don't explain I know you'll go away,
But try as I might, there's no meeting of minds
So I'm writing between the lines.

I'm writing between the lines on a page,
But words can't describe the madness, the rage,
The impulsion that made me spend one night with him;
I'll have to go out on a limb.

I'll have to go out on a limb, and blame you,
And my mother, my schooldays, the first man I knew,
Or the fact I'm in touch with my masculine side –
But I won't take you for a ride.

I won't take you for a ride, or a fool,
'Cause I know that you're burning, although you act cool,
And I've damaged your pride, and sullied your name,
And it's just not playing the game.

And I wasn't playing the game, or the field,
Or mending old wounds that never quite healed;
I can't even pretend that it's only fair
That you've done what I did, you've had your share;
In that spontaneous moment, I just didn't care –
It's the same motivation makes mountaineers dare –
I did it because he was there.

Somewhere to love
or
Don't carp over coyness
We made love in the morning under an awning, out on the grass;
And once on a train the emergency chain was pulled, as we fucked
      (second class);
We screwed up the stairway to heaven, and seven times more
      on the floor;
And when you were able we laid on the table, served each other
      till we were raw;
In a wood we embarrassed the aspens, till they shivered
      with prurient glee;
And the salt water prickled and tickled, as we pickled ourselves
      in the sea;
There were marks on your back from the carpet, when our flames
      matched the logfire burning,
And on dark windy nights we flew wild kites of love, and we swore
      we could feel the world turning;
In an alley we climaxed at midnight, my right hand caressing a cat,
But when lust started flowering while you watched me showering –
Well, I must draw the line at that.
And I'm not a prude, that's just not the case,
I only think loving deserves its due space,
When your bum's on the plug, hot and cold up your spine, please,
Where d'you put elbows and knees?
The bath's a fine but private place,
And none, I think, should there embrace.

Prometheus
The next poem that I write
Will have you in it –
The honesty of your back, perhaps;
Your misbehaving smile, or weeping hair.

The next poem that I write
Will have you in it –
It might have classic themes,
Of love or lightning, death,
Or ageless vegetation;
You'll be there.

The next poem that I write
Will have you in it.
It might be about politics or war;
But you're the stones and sticks
I build upon; the bones
My metric muscles cling to;
The audience I sing to,
With your hammer and your roses
And your fire in every line –
My Prometheus!

The next poem that I write
Will not be mine.

More
Sing me a sad song!
Show me how you feel;
Tell me that love isn't real,
That you're fucked up inside your head;
You sit and stare at an empty bed;
And even your fucking dog is dead,
And no-one seems to care;
Just give me what you want to share
And, baby, I'll be there.

Come to me with a sad proposal;
I'm just a misery waste disposal,
With a blind eye for your vilest sin;
I'll soothe your mind and save your skin –
Just throw your dogshit in my bin –
That's all that I'm here for.
And so what if I'm scarred and sore?
I'll just come back for more.

My Achilles

You sit high-handed in your great black ship,
Pointing seaward, but beached high on the shore.
You've taken your ball in, and refuse
To join the game of war.

I send emissaries: love-notes, roses,
Promises to give back all the things I owe;
But you sit high-handed, sulking, in your ship.
You just don't want to know.

What will it take to make you grab your sword,
Challenge Apollo's light, leave your shield behind?
So what if we die together, facing battle?
I wouldn't mind.

Red daffodils

When daffodils blaze like a post-office van,
And February skies show nothing but blue;
When monkfish tails pray as they're fried in a pan,
And facts can be graded as more or less true;
When the worst cars are those that are made in Japan,
And post-it notes stick with the strongest of glue;
When a Goth can admit he's a funky house fan,
And the French understand how to wait in a queue;
When governments slap on a *no*-smoking ban,
And weeding can feel like a fun thing to do –
That's when I'll stop wanting you as my man,
'Cause I just can't help loving you.

Cats' eyes

As fragile as the road's cats' eyes;
As casual as black bow ties;
As shamefaced as last summer's lies;
As welcome as the second prize –
That's unrequited love.

As well-built as a cuckoo's nest;
As comfy as a woollen vest;
As certain as the Grail's quest;
As shy as a gatecrashing guest –
It's uninvited love.

As unrepeatable as spring,
As gentle as a hornet's sting;
As measurable as a piece of string;
As blind as eagles on the wing –
It's just shortsighted love.

But there it is. What can I do?
You fit me like a handmade shoe,
Or Inca bricks; don't need the glue
Of deathless declarations. Who
Dares say it's not enough for two?
For strong and shameless, bold and true
With a clear and unobstructed view;
No fear; unlocked, delighted love
Is what I feel for you.

Ferry
There was a time
When sleepslip thoughts
Were of his body, skin
To skin with mine;
And waking neurones fired
Off smiles.
But that's
All gone now. Tired
To death, one phrase alone is in
My mind; it sails
Through shipwrecked dreams;
A jagged ferry, plying
One sad trade,
One life unmade; and, lying,
Eyes closed, all I see
Is this: it seems
He doesn't love me.
He doesn't love me.
He doesn't love me.

Accident
The day has had an accident.
I witness it, from my car-parked
Passenger seat. Driven
By words from him behind the wheel,
Minutes veer into verges,
Hours overturn;
Skies skid,
Clouds collide,
And rain crashes down my cheeks;
And I am immobilised;
Brakes off; broken.

Sleep now
Sleep now.
Curl yourself,
Comma'd as a cat.
Place carefully the tail you do not have
Before your eyes,
And know that in night's forest,
Where all things are in disguise,
One tree stands firm;
One truth remains;
One hand holds fast,
When all is dark.

Sleep now.
From death to morning light
Is only a small stretch,
A stroll through shadow,
A whisker's twitch;
A pause.

Dangerous sports
Dangerous sports? I've done them all –
Cliff-diving; bungee; parachute (freefall).
But nothing scares me more than this:
The fear of pain in every kiss.

Not in charge
Once, suspected drunks were told
To walk along a painted line.
I am intoxicated now.
My feet slip out from under me.
My vision's blurred; my thoughts are slurred;
I feel I'm being tested.
I try to walk a line of words
That will keep you arrested,
Though I'm the one who's guilty,
And I don't want to be free.

Sleeping
Like a dog dreaming,
He twitches as he falls asleep,
And I want him to keep falling.
Like a cat, he curls awake,
Cautious of the day,
And I want him to stay.
Like the best of days, he's bright,
Burning deep into soft nights
Until they gleam,
And I want him to dream.
Like dreams, he's shy.
His laughter hides what's real;
And I want him to feel
That I'm his bed, his hiding place,
His fur to stroke; the smiling face
That when he's falling wants to help him fly.
He twitches, and he touches me; and sleeping dogs don't lie.

Sensible
I know I must be sensible.
I have to drive away
And go back to the everyday,
The every night all-rightness.
But this sense seems reprehensible:
To turn my back on brightness,
Switch the spotlights of a passion
For the slight flame of a candle –
It's more than my heart can handle,
Or my mind can rationalise;
And my hands, my tongue, my ears, my eyes –
All my senses – tell me; the evidence is strong:
That though leaving you is sensible,
It's wrong.

Pockets
It is to be expected
That a man who adopts cats
Shelters small creations, casually collected,
In his pockets: a hat
That mutates into a ruff;
Enough tissues for a different life;
A foreskinned umbrella, frightened of the dry;
The shy hedgehog of a Swiss army knife,
Bristles retracted; a shape-shifting bag, compacted.
Dressed, he is functional,
But with messages mixed as fingerless mittens
Or sabre-toothed kittens.

He rarely bares his skin
To let outsiders in,
But when at last he is unwrapped
And naked, lapped by a bedsheet sea
And swimming next to me,
Unratcheted and gadget-free,
With no pockets of resistance
In his mind –
That's when I hope that he can find
The real object of existence.

La petite mort (2)
The French, as always, got it wrong,
Although they seem so sure,
When they used the phrase
La petite mort –
The little death –
To indicate the deepest breath
Of orgasm.
For me, it is the chasm
In my heart,
The Grand Canyon's rim I walk along,
Every time we part.

Tower Bridge
Look at Tower
Bridge. When flat, it's
giving power,
doing business,
making crossings,
stitching regions.
Pointing up, it's
impotent, a
symbol of man's
skill; no more.
                    But
between us two
a bridge, rising,
engineered by
liquid forces –
sucking lips and
licking tongues and
strange hydraulics;
lubricated
by a listing
lust that lifts it,
stuffed and lofty –
this bridge brings our
banks together;
joins our ranks and
flanks together;
closes gaps and
turns on taps and
makes us cry out
Gods be thanked!
                    and
when it falls, its
work completed,
triumphant, but
now depleted –
us repleted,
then its function's
more straightforward.

Symbolism's
most important.
When I think of
Tower Bridge, my
mind's eye sees it
up.

La petite mort
La petite mort, it's called in French;
Each petty triumph or surrender
Acts as just a benchmark
For the senses' end;
Each vulnerable disclosure
Posed to represent
The ultimate exposure of the soul;
The violence of conception
A perception of the cancerous attack
Or wound or rupture; the flak
Of life that penetrates and kills;
That finishes as it fulfils.

So afterwards, complete and lying
Together
About eternity,
The truth is – we are dying.

Trapeze

If I were flying high on a trapeze,
I would trust you to stretch my safety net.
If I were struggling to pay my fees,
I know you'd bail me out, and then forget
All that I owe. If I were blind,
You'd hold my hand and always take the lead.
You would cook for me each day, and never mind
That all my offerings are burned. I never need
To shed a tear unnoticed; you're aware
Of each shiver and each shudder; every sigh
Gives you an opportunity to show you care.
And when you wake, you smile at me. So why
Is this not love? You try, but just can't say,
And high on my trapeze, the ground seems very far away.
Why is this not love? You talk, but don't explain;
The trapeze artist becomes a clown, again.

The knack

I seem to have lost the knack
Of sleeping alone.
Where is that welcoming back,
The comforting groan
Of the snores that I thought I'd despise?
Where are those eyes
That smile, full of sleep?
Where is that arm that keeps creeping around me?
Here, only sheets surround me. They lack,
Well, just about all that I like.
You'd think it would be like riding a bike –
One night alone and I'd be back on track –
But no. I have quite lost the knack.
It seems I need you in the sack.

Damped

Quiet now.
No piston-pumping pounding,
No smell of smoke or passion,
Just a private joke, a passing smile;
It's a while since this meant more than
Children's stories;
The door is shut on these fairytales,
With romance remote on the other side;
Life's inevitable rails
Come in between,
Other priorities intervene,
Though the silent running doesn't hide
The loss of this earlier dream –
Our love, like the locomotives,
Has just run out of steam.

Gap

The tooth, extracted twenty years ago,
Has left no gap.
Molars moved like moss;
Closed ranks; redrew the map;
Obliterated history.

But
Though the space where you once were
Is closing slowly, it remains,
Probed every aching day by the mystery
Of memory, sensitive as complaining tongue
To roughened edges, ulcered pain,
And the knowledge of what's missing.
It is a space once shaped by kissing.

Folding time

If I could fold myself in half
Then I could hide the hurt at the heart,
Show just the shiny outer cover.
But, knowing my lover,
There would soon be another pain;
I'd have to fold myself again.

Now, why don't you try this at home?
Take some paper, fold in two,
Twice; three times; again; it gets
Much harder. You will find it's true –
Somehow, the laws of physics state
There is a maximum of eight
Times anything can be folded double;
It seems our relationship's in trouble
Because this is a given.
Today my lover made me cry,
So it's folding time once more; I'll try,
But the count's already seven.

Tightrope

I'm high; I'm wired;
No longer tired,
But fired with feelings I'd mislaid.
I'm caught; I'm taut as any tightrope,
Full of hope
But so afraid –
I have forgotten how it's done,
Love's balancing act of fear and fun;
One foot astray, one word untrue
And gravity will take its due,
But one thing's worth the risk: it's you.

I don't want to write this poem
It is too ordinary, this;
The coldness of lips turned away from a kiss;
The brevity of phone calls,
Which once went on for hours,
The clichéd lack of present flowers –
There's nothing new to say,
And I don't want to write this poem today
About how it feels when love goes away;
It would just be full of curses,
Or empty; no more than blank verses.

A chair
A relationship that's like a chair is not worth sitting on, she said.
He thought they were comfortable together.
A man who behaves like a pavement is not worth spitting on, she said.
He was prostrating himself at her feet.
An embrace that holds too hard is suffocating, she said.
He was protecting her from the world.
If you never act, you'll spend your whole life waiting, she said -
And yes, he would, for ever, on her, hand and foot.
When love is dead the kiss of life is wasted, she said.
He wanted to cover her with kisses.
No life's complete till bitterness is tasted, she said.
But he would have fed her endlessly on sweetness.

Washing

Once, there was a reckless heap of clothes left where they dropped -
My blouse embraced your underwear, your shirt fondled my bra -
But now there's just two tidy piles. The clothes, like us, have stopped
Their hugging and their intimacy; now they are
Self-contained, and private. The abandon that they shared before
Has gone; all that remains is dirty washing on the floor.

Last night she hugged me

Last night I dreamt she hugged me,
Slipped in through the door, and
Straight into my arms, the
Daughter who I lost those years ago;
Her warm hair smooth against my cheek,
The smell of her, known only to a mother,
Stronger than the candles I'd left burning;
Her body, solid as the pillow, pressed close
Against me, filling the awful gap
Which I've surrounded with an empty life.

Last night I dreamt she hugged me.
It was so real, the feel of her,
Far more real than your embrace,
So now I cannot bear your arms around me.
I need to keep her here with me,
This emotion is – yes, a virtual reality;
If I close my eyes, she is here still;
My other senses tell more truth
Than my reason-blinded eyes can see.

It will fade, no doubt.
Physical dreams last longer than mere images,
But never long enough,
And soon she will be gone,
Even from the night's imagination,
With no lingering vibration
From this now tangible echo.

Please leave me until then,
Your touch disturbs my body's memory,
And you'll be here long after she has gone.
Let me retain this most-missed bliss,
Just a moment more, just a day,
Just a week, if I can keep it close,
And lodged in my life's patterns.
Her imprint on my skin would be erased by your caress,
And smell and sound by the waves of your kind voice would be
        washed clear.

Don't touch, don't talk, and then perhaps she'll hear -
Please stay with me, my girl, my love,
        don't go, don't go, don't go.....

6th Street, Austin

Friday night on 6th Street;
And a woman with a sequinned bag and bare feet
Sits a spit away
From bars of blaring sound,
The places where the people play;
And girls in crotch-tight jeans
Know what it means
When guys look round
As they pass by.
And the biggish woman selling gyros
Gyrates to the radio's old songs,
Keeps the beat with a pack of Marlboro,
Tapped against her wrist;
A tall transvestite in a thong
Displays his ass and shakes his fist,
And the creamy coffee-coloured men
Are substitutes for caffeine
For the unseen woman, all alone,
Who walks up and down, again and again,
Looking.
Outside Vibe it's cooking.
Simmering shimmering kids
Wait for the lid to pop,
The show to start,
But cool it, move apart
For an ambulance to pass.
The radio advert's selling
Laser therapy for hairy backs,
And pizza makes for half-moon snacks,
And a couple in smart slacks and tweed
Stay near the cops, who need
Root beer and diet coke
For fuel, and like an enemy's telescope
Are mounted on dark horses or black bikes.
The unseen woman has a smoke –
Not the brand she likes –
And looks,
And loves the lack of homogeneity,
The mathematical variety
Of seed and breed and need and greed and deed.

She waits, and writes,
And lights another cigarette,
Not ready to go yet;
And, with nothing much to lose,
She buys a sequinned bag, and smiles,
And then
Takes off her shoes.

Notes: 6th Street, Austin is full of bars with live music. Vibe is one of these bars. A gyro is a filled baguette.

Victoria coach station, 5 a.m.

It's just a small hole in my life,
This hour spent waiting for a bus:
Victoria, five a.m.

On perforated metal seats,
Fixed to the floor, no chance of change,
Sit punctured people: silent, snoring;
A mother with a sleeping child
And yellow skirt; a baggaged couple
Parted by a ledge that holds no coffee;
Backpackers, coming back or packing off –
Who knows? And everybody who arrives
Goes first to see the corner labelled *Toilets* –
And turns back, disappointed, bladder-wracked,
Confronted by a locked and vacant gate:
No openings for engagement.
And no-one speaks.
No conversations stitch a seam
Between us. Our only point of contact
Is the row of perforated seats,
Inevitably painted the same grey as this small hole in my life,
And as the sky outside Victoria, five a.m.

Airport, Terminal 1
A tall man in a boiler suit;
Cap on backwards, workman's boots.
A girl, relaxed, with turned-up jeans.
They meet, and kiss – what can this mean?
She has a case; she's been away –
He hasn't. He is here to stay.
An airport worker, I would guess.
They drink their coffees; smile; caress.
I'm privileged to be here, just when
They finally meet up again,
And see this moment of pure joy –
The old story of a girl and boy.

Cliff face
Lived in.
It's what they say of faces,
But it's true of places, too.
This old Greek island cliff has seen it all.
Beneath a tangled mop of twisted olives,
Wars have driven frowns into its brow.
Around the craggy eyes the years of peering
Out to sea have riven wrinkles.
Sagging rockfalls jowl its crumbling chin,
But rising crinkles, sandstone strata,
Show the signs of centuries
Of nights drunk on red wine and raucous laughter.
It rests its tired body in the waves,
Limbs relaxed in atavistic comfort,
With just one rocky finger raised and pointing
At history, and memories, and the sea.

Accents

The accents grope the ancient air,
Pawing at its peace.
Scouse drawls through its underwear;
Manchester's lumpy hand has no finesse.
Essex howls sour nothings in its ear.
Scandinavian lilts a soft caress.
Germanic undoes all its zips.
French strips it with an arrogance.
Grecian honey coats its lips;
Italian tries, but fails, romance,
While I plan silent, buttoned-lip seduction.
But behind these stereotypical tones
Sound syllables of instruction:
The waves seduce with a language of their own.

Clean

It must be big enough, the sea,
to wash away anything.
Millions of dead fish,
for a start. Weed,
well past its sell-by date,
like cucumber left in a fridge. Wee:
thousands of holidaymakers,
this island alone.
The contents of ships' bins,
no doubt, regulations broken.
Fear. Pain. Memories. Sins.
So I take off all my clothes,
and swim.

Cheek

It seems to me as natural as drinking,
When I am on a beach, warm-washed and Greek,
To stop worrying what my mother would be thinking
And spend each hour, each day of my short week
Naked, as humanity was intended
To go about its business, free from care
And clothing. Look how fig-leaf fashion's ended,
In such fuss about the petty rags we wear.

And if I seem to be on the defensive,
It's another natural feeling showing through:
I know my skin can be, to some, offensive;
Stripping off can seem the rudest thing to do,
In, say, wet and windy Wales, when you're antique:
It's effrontery – no more than bare-faced cheek.

Kitten

We saw it moving by the wall.
Road-maim, perhaps, or blown black plastic;
A lizard of rubbish; a discarded crawl.
But nearer, it was tragic, drastic,
Mewing, doing all it could
To stay alive, furry half-baked legs
As impotent as driftwood,
Straining blindly in the gritty tide. Now, it begs
Unknowingly to be held, protected.
We try. We stroke, and gentle.
Kitten urine dribbles, almost undetected
On our hands' despairing mantle.

It would need feeding every hour.
There is a house nearby with cats.
This one will surely die, and our
Heads tell us we should leave it. That's
What we do. But this pathetic
Flotsam of a life has blessed our skin;
The certainty of its end seems distantly prophetic
Of our own. So, for a while, we mourn our kin.

Ramble

I'm going on a ramble –
An aimless amble through some ragged brambles
And the untamed flowers.
It will take hours
To walk two miles.
The thought does not beguile
Me.
A walk should be a preamble
To postcard views or kite-like climbs;
A scramble over tumbled rocks;
A race against geology's jumbled clocks.
Stopping at each blooming herb –
Time after thyme after oregano after sage –
Does not belong on my hike's page;
It should be a tale of verbs,
Not adjectives.
A walk should have objectives;
You should feel nerves and muscles biting;
Like fine writing.
I would with a will gamble
Anything, that Shakespeare never went on a ramble.

Sea shelves

Seaside shopping
Sales are dropping –
Goods are slowly going bad:
Bottles musty,
Packets dusty –
Supermarket shelves look sad.

While beached and roasted,
Bleached and toasted,
Rows of bodies dehydrate;
Almost bare,
Without a care,
Hastening their sell-by date.

On nights like these

On nights like these
When distant lightning
Slakes the starless
Skies, and unheard
Thunder threatens
Thought;
On nights like these,
When love is dead,
Only the sea
Can answer questions,
With a delphic
Simile – deep as,
Wide as, dark as
Casual anger, and regret.
I sit and wish,
On nights like these,
For endings; far
Too many starts
Have phosphoresced
And falsified.
On nights like these
The music that
I want to hear
Is silent.

Wave goodbye

A floating flower, bobbing pinkly
On Aegean waves
Does not behave
As you'd expect:
It's not washed in,
To spoil the gesture of throwing it,
But, as if lackadaisically rowing, it
Drifts, along and out;
Lifts and falls, unrhythmically;
Falters; appears to hesitate, come back,
But alters course again.
There can be no return;
But then, there is no end.

Nothing on
This week, I've had nothing on:
No dates to keep,
No sleep split by alarms,
No anxious qualms about what I am doing,
No to-ing and fro-ing, one task to the next,
No texts or emails,
No failure to keep up with all the jobs around my garden and my home;
Only cards and poems to write.
I have become a creature of the night:
A cat. I stroll and eat and stalk;
I sometimes play, and rarely talk;
I doze just when I want to, and I purr.
But, best of all,
This week I have had nothing on;
Not even fur.
And when you have as many clothes as me,
Then only nakedness can set you free.

Just for me
Two goat bells play a minor third.
Lonely dogs howl in the hills,
And cicadas chirp because they have no choice.
The alarm cocks do their job,
And the old man from the house across the path
Shuffles to the downstairs bathroom,
Takes a leak, leaving the door open.
Cats are fighting somewhere, crying
Like babies in the dark.
The night world moans at morning,
But from my high Greek balcony,
Where I am drinking pre-dawn tea, I see
Only stars, hand-painted;
And I know the sun will rise soon,
Just for me.

Something of Greece

He asks me for a poem that holds something of Greece.
Of course, I'll write it down in blue;
But how should I convey the ancient peace
Of endless sunshine, the stark clarity
Of the light, the charity
Shown to strangers by its people?

My lines should have the texture
Of warm honey, and must resonate with resin;
But I find my words too feeble
For the persistence of percussion
Of soft waves against hard rock,
Each one echoing the clash of far-off fights.
How can I get it right?
I cannot argue well enough;
Even my punctuation fails;
Each stop and semi-colon
Should invite an hour's discussion;
And each consonant's too rough
For a language pressed from olives,
And slid across the sea by languid sails.

And – how to end?
With the bitterness of coffee,
Or a bout of bad philosophy?
No: with a promise that, to get this poem perfect,
I'm going to have to taste it all again.
And again. And again. And again. And again.

Plastic explosive

The plastic bottle, full of Coke,
Kept safely plastic-bagged within my holdall,
Seemed quite harmless. So I thought,
Until the first twist of its plastic lid stopped short
My drinking plans, as it went pop!
And flew, ridiculously high,
Above an ageing German couple sunbathing nearby,
And landed on the pebbles with a plop.
My Siegfried hobbled off across the stones,
Before I had a chance to get some
Sandals, and sought it, stepping gingerly,
Barefoot; brought it back, this small red jetsam;
Presented it with a bow and this short speech:
It should have been champagne.
And so, on this unfriendly beach,
Two nations waged a little peace campaign.

My offering

The bread is dry and rough against my tongue,
As if the sand that sunbathes round the island
Left off loafing in the ovens of the beaches
To be baked properly.
The feta hits my throat just like
The spray I choked on yesterday;
Mouthfuls, flung in fury by a sea
Resentful of the fast boat's battering.
But the tomato – oh, the tomato!
How unlike Edam's is its skin!
How is the sun stored as such sweet
Acidity? I don't know.

It's just another sandwich, I suppose;
One more slice of life.
But this is Greece,
And who could ask for more?
I trickle careful crumbs on the balcony floor:
My offering.

Easy prey
I am on holiday alone.
I think alone, I drink alone,
I turn from pale to pink alone,
With no-one to rub lotion on my back.
I am the solitary mule, bearing as big a pack as I am able.
I am the silent, staring fool, shrinking at the
Only one-chaired table
In the overlit café, where I am easy prey,
A ready target for the waiter,
Who asks me for my order, for my name, and whether
        I will meet him later,
When his shift has ended.
I could be tempted;
But, instead, I buy cards for the phone,
And make a call: an answering machine.
And so I talk alone;
And, all unseen, I walk alone
To my double-bedded room,
Where I drink alone, and think alone,
And before I get a chance to weep,
I go to sleep,
Alone.

Entropy
It started off quite neat –
Sandals tucked beneath the seat,
Hopeful skirts hung, waiting, on the rail,
Each item in its place.
But, slowly, I have left a trail,
And everything that was in my case
Is strewn around at random,
The spare bed blanketed with books
And carrier bags; a pandem-
Onium of packets, underwear, and shoes.
It's all my mess, and I confess it looks
As if I'd nothing left to lose.
If my mind was like this, I would need therapy,
But, actually, it's deliberate –
I want to demonstrate the law of entropy.

Ten different kinds of nothing

1

The dull grey
Of clouds over a Greek beach,
Taking away
All purpose from a holiday.

2

The numb promise
Of a writer's blank page.

3

The young blonde affair
Marking a man's middle age.

4

The absence that there was,
Or perhaps wasn't, before the mighty bang
Which, we are told, rang
In, or out, the universe.

5

The emptiness that follows, without fail,
The words: *for better or for worse* -
There is no good or bad, just mediocre.

6

The expression on the face
Of the one who wins at poker.

7

The powerlessness of being really,
And I mean pennilessly, skint.

8

The centre of a doughnut,
Or hula hoop, or polo mint.

9

The calm of smallness
Faced with a vast and busy sea.

10

Me.

Village idiot
Past hippo rocks,
Through shoals of iron filings;
Surgically enhanced by plastic tubing.
I play the clumsy dolphin –
Inefficient fins befrog me.
But this is Greece, where
Every village tolerates its idiot,
And where myths and wonders live.
I can believe these waters are my home.

When a butterfly lands
When a butterfly lands
On a sandwich-supporting finger,
No brakes scream,
No rubber burns,
No uniforms flick switches,
And no seat-belts are unclipped,
But time stops,
Just long enough
For the tapestry of upright wings to be admired,
For the finger to know privilege,
For nearby watchers to feel envy;
For the skin's warm tarmac to capture the impression
And keep it.

My octopus bed *or* **Holiday plans**
My octopus bed
Won't let me go.
It fills my head
With lead and snow.
I lift a limb –
It flops and drops.
I want to swim
Or hit the shops,
But all, it seems,
I do is drowse
In deep-sea dreams
For hours and hours.

Intelligent design
A nudist beach: men's bits on show, a-dangle, or stuck out;
And bosoms – so untidy as they bounce and flop about.
This lack of streamlined elegance leaves very little doubt.
Essential elements, exposed, are vulnerable and sad;
And the proponents of intelligent design? They must be mad.

The effects of a Mediterranean climate on nocturnal behaviour
Late night: a Mediterranean town:
The voltas, ramblas – up and down
They walk – the Greeks and Brits and Scands,
Pushing pushchairs, holding hands.
The lonely sit and watch them go,
Wishing that they too could know
The pleasure to be gained from walking
Aimlessly, and sometimes talking.
Why then this ceaseless, lazy storm?
Because they can; because it's warm.

Conundrum
It is an old conundrum:
Two boys fall in filth, then see each other;
The clean one goes to wash his face.
So, I sit on the beach,
And watch – long limbs, unwrinkled skin,
Athletic grace;
And lie back, smiling, in my place,
Fat thighs a-quiver;
While they –
They look at me,
And shiver.

Kefalonian vistas

It looks like Scarborough.
The people might be browner,
But the clouds are still a downer;
The view may be Ionian –
Distant vistas Kefalonian,
Not tankers;
But they're British tourists here,
Old men with cigarettes and beer,
Or wankers
Shouting in the street,
Offending everyone they meet,
And the weather's dull and grey.
This isn't why I came on holiday.
A Greek week all alone is
When you hope to meet Adonis;
Not a retired Yorkshire pair
With permed, blue-rinsed or thinning hair,
Whose only chat is grandchildren and cruises.
And low-price, limitless booze is
Not the reason why I came.
No. Just the same
As these families with pre-school kids
I wanted sunshine, cheap.
But the clouds have put a lid under the heat
And turned the sea deep
Grey.
This isn't why I came on holiday.
I want the blue, the turquoise and the gold;
I want some strong brown foreign arms to hold
Me; and I want them now, before I grow too old.

Time to go

Time to go.
Time to brush off sand and gather in
The flotsam of a day spent at the beach;
Add the jetsam to the drifts of bags and
Cans and empty bottles;
Slog up the slopes and through the
Scruffy pines where all the week
A donkey has been tethered.
Though not today;
Hear the seal honk of the bus, waiting,
And run the last descent, bags bouncing
Like the little boats in the ferry's wake;
Say thank you to the driver
For not just doing his job;
Stare through streaky windows and
Capture the last glimpses of the sea,
As if a shoal of coelacanths has surfaced;
Push through the gently swaying
Seaweed passengers, to swim free at stop 16;
Fumble for the treasure of a neatly hidden key;
Unlock the door, my door;
And shower; and dress; and eat;
And pack.

But first, one final poem,
To be written in salt water.
I will call it:
Time to go.

Wireless
I heard it on the radio,
An age of two whole days ago –
The unseen dj said *Hello!*
And sent out unfelt wishes;
And here I am, a flight away,
Where crickets sing and dolphins play.
I haven't heard the news all day –
I'm swimming with the fishes.

I skip through waves, instead of stations;
Converse by sign with all the nations;
I'm feeling frequently elation,
And sampling different dishes.
Football, budgets – who cares here?
I'm wireless now, my airwaves clear,
And till my programme's end is near,
I'm swimming with the fishes.

In the Greek way
We're here on the Aegean, or perhaps the Adriatic,
Sitting on the Doric coast, though possibly it's Attic.
My knowledge of geography is really very weak,
But I know I'm not alone, and here beside me is a Greek.

He's talking in a language that I barely understand,
Emphasising every word with a gesture of his hand.
Little bits I recognise, at least I think I do,
And his meaning is as clear as the Aegean (or possibly the Adriatic)
        is blue.

And when I met him on the beach, I must have got it wrong.
He was oiled and tanned and perfect, and wearing just a thong,
And I thought I knew exactly what he was trying to say –
That I'd be safe with him tonight, 'cos after all he's gay.

But if he's gay I'm a sunhat made of cheap and fraying straw.
I know what he's after; I've been here before.
I need to find an exit route, after what I'm sure he said –
The gay Greek god beside me just asked me to his bed.

172

Photograph
Across the bay a dozen tiny comets
Rise eternally to seek each personal moon.
In my right ear, American voices
Laugh over a sitcom's opening tune.
Brave in the dark, a solitary firefly darts
As if on ice, to a cartoon collision.
Fat northerners to my left sit down,
Light cigarettes, chat with a soap's precision.

Our perfect waiter knows what's what, and
Before we even ask, says *With two spoons.*
It is ten pm, and twenty-five degrees; Skiathos,
On this final day of June.
Far below sound sleigh bells. No snow here,
But horse-drawn carriages, waiting for a fare.
An apricot moon is shy of being pictured,
And we will never prove that it was there.
My failures with the camera make me cross,
But he is patient, quietly starts to laugh.
I'm unsteady; all is blurred. I do it this way –
These words must serve me as a photograph.

Not required

No poem is needed.
No words are required.
This is how things are,
And I am not inspired.

A small dose of anguish
Is all it would take,
But I don't want pain
Just for poetry's sake.

You carry my stuff,
And I massage your feet.
We hunt crabs together
And share what we eat.

We smile when we wake;
Hold close when we're tired.
It's all how it should be.
No poems required.

Kilimanjaro

The day before the summit
there is a long plain.
You can see where you will be tomorrow,
and only slow steps in thin air, pain,
between. You borrow
a solitary boulder's shelter,
and defecate where every other walker
has shat before you.
Slow-motion skelter-helter,
inevitable anti-gravity, you climb.
You have tried to cover yourself
but unexpected burn
hits unprotected, forgotten parts this time –
ears, hand-backs, nose-tip.
Inside is a still chill.
And the peak stuns. You learn
why, for one moment,
and then it's all downhill.

Weymouth
You see it all down here.
Two fat ladies, walking hand in hand.
A swaggering man, with a tiny dog.
A young couple lost in a fog of love.
A plastic shovel handle, sticking out of the sand,
Abandoned by a toddler, and tearfully missed.
Four young men, snoring; pissed.
Beach-ball girls, bouncing in the breeze,
Shunning everyone with the middle-age disease.
A solitary goth, eclipsed by the sun.
Trampoline muscles, out for a run.
Disappointed surfers, with their dolphin skins,
Stranded on the shoreline, flapping their fins.
Overflowing bins, favours and sins,
Flavours and smells, tram-car bells,
Hard rock and candy floss and scattered shells...
The peace of the sea seems out of reach,
But otherwise, I guess, life's a beach.

Gates of fire
On days like this
Greek warriors gave their lives
Where now bulk pensioners in winter sunshine bask,
Knowing nothing of the past,
And descendants of the Spartans argue, smiling;
Whiling away aeons in coffee shop philosophy.
But I am waiting for a train.
A chilly pause in a life fuelled by no cause
Worth dying for, or trying for, even; just the pain
Of paying bills. But the sun, the February sun
Takes me to shores where cobalt fills
My north sea eyes, kills
Cares; where freedom was begun
With battles, and set on rails to terminate in
The peaceful slavery of this English shire,
Where, in my overcoated armour,
I must catch a train and travel to
A meeting, when I'd really rather be with those
Who guarded gates of fire.

Shocked and surprised
I was shocked and surprised when he talked about
New worlds.
A metaphor, I thought at first, but no:
He really meant it. *Let's go,*
He said. I'd seen him as a rich guy
With a hobby - astronomy, the sky,
Galaxies, all of that; not my thing -
One little room is an everywhere to me.
The world will end at lunchtime,
He remarked, as if were an everyday occurrence.
Let us possess a new one.
I put my scorn in my pocket,
With my bus ticket,
And followed him, not being one to miss
An opportunity. And there it was - a rocket.
I climbed in.

That was yesterday. And now,
Good morning to my waking soul -
I am a passenger; he is in control
Of where we go, and what we see -
The hemispheres below (not ended yet),
The stars above.

All I expected, when I put on my green hat
And my nicest underwear, before our date,
Was that we'd make love.

Well, it's a start...
I might move into the sun...
I'll try worms....
That bloke on the Humber, he swore by vegetables...
God, I hate this clay.
I bet it's been here since before the floods,
You know, a few years back.
That's when that iron gate arrived,
Washed down, riding the surge
Like some mad chariot.
I've never been one for tearing pleasures, myself.
Sit down; think which way to walk;
Pass the long day...
That's me.
But it's dragging today;
It feels like a hundred years have gone
For just two small fish.
An age at least to every carp.
Still, I promised.
I've done what I can.
It would take me eternity to rustle up dessert;
Can't do them fast.
This'll have to do then.
Just reach into the ashes -
Good. Still warm. Five loaves.

Shamed

You embarrassed me, that time;
Five feet one, no wider than a secondhand;
My mother.

It was bad enough
That you were there at all, in London, with me;
I had planned to come alone.

Night-time, Leicester Square.
One man picked on another, started punching.
You waded in.

"Leave him alone!"
With the authority of a ref, you stood your ground.
They moved apart,

Eyes down, sullen,
Put in their places by a featherweight,
And I - I turned away,

Shamed by a parent,
Because she acted - or because I didn't?
I'll never know.

Then

Grannies. Grannies died young, then;
They didn't linger on for years,
Clinging to a lifeline of false teeth,
Home helps, whinging and wheelchairs.

And schools. Schools were the truce
Of life; a brief pause between the wars
That parents waged on shellshocked children;
Dinner ladies the mothers we never had.

And work. Work was secure as bank vaults,
And as lively, with everything in its place,
And a bullion waiting when retirement slammed
The door, shortly before you died.

Oh, it was all so much better then,
With time to watch the sun traverse
         the green moquette
On Sundays; an absence of grannies,
Insecurity, adventure, spirit; all killed by war.

Indifference - a reply to Wilfred Owen

Yes, I woke cold stars, cold clay.
Each life, each death belongs to me.
Each home, each field, the sunbeams' play,
Each atom that you cannot see,
Each molecule and universe,
Each earthy grub and soul divine.
Who are you to beg and curse?
Indifference, too, is mine.

Beetling

In some untidy corner,
Full of leaf mould and old wood,
A scratching horse provides an earthquake,
And a bee the hum of death;
And blossom from the almond tree
Falls with surprise and pinkish rain;
And puddles mean the risk of drowning,
Sun the certainty of pain,
Easing only with the autumn.

In this untidy corner,
A rifle bolt cracks like a twig,
And shouted orders roar like ants,
And war's no more than distant thunder;
Ceasefire might as well be myth,
Long lost to human knowledge, which,
In this beetle's case, it has not got.

How do I love you?

Let me count the ways:
Enough to rub your feet on Sundays;
Not enough to wash your underwear.
Enough to share a toothbrush;
Not enough to rush to meet you.
Enough to treat you when it's not my turn;
Not enough to tell you just how much I earn.
Enough to do the washing up;
Not enough to do it in the way you like.
Enough to keep my bike in your shed;
Not enough to give up my own bed.
Enough to live with, in my ageing years;
Not enough to live with you.

Mucky swans

Swans! we said, in unison, as icebergs of white feather
showed bright across the estuary.
A mob; twenty or more; but falling closer,
they were not what we'd expected.
Porcelain heads; beaks like golden handles;
but with a tidemark as in a sink
when the washing up is done;
below the petals of their wings
was nothing more than muck.

Our bright day faded at the sight;
as if the moon that whitens trees
wore dirty underwear,
or a young girl's sweet hair
crawled with lice.

We turned our backs
and picked our way in silence to the car;
mud squelched beneath the shingle.
They mate for life, you said,
and we both wondered if
it might be better to stay single.

We did

If the sun had not been as seductive as Andrew Marvell,
I wouldn't have worn that dress.

If I hadn't been in raven and poppies,
The colours of revolution,
You might not have taken a shine,
Polished the surfaces of your charm.

If you hadn't sparkled like the bubbles in your beer,
I wouldn't have knocked it over,
Shying like a thoroughbred.

If either of us had been better bred,
We wouldn't have swapped looks
Like sandwiches from lunchboxes;
Eaten each other up.

If neither of us had been hungry,
We would have been well satisfied.

If we had known what was good for us,
We would have left the table,
Not stayed until the pub caught fire,
Which it really did, but not until
After we had been burned
By each other's poetry, seductive as Andrew Marvell.

But as it was,
We did.

Never Prufrock

I don't do flannel; not my thing at all;
But every year I hear the mermaids call,
And have to make my way down to the sea.
A ragged pair of claws he might have been; not me –
I swim like yellow smoke that rubs and slides;
He is a self-conscious fool; besides,
He's going bald. He's not the man I thought;
I never liked the bracelets that he bought,
Or the way he leered at my white arms.
I'm sure he never meant me any harm,
But oh, the boring nights in cheap hotels,
His coffee spoon obsession, and the shells
Of oysters he found fascinating.
He'd stare at them for hours, while I stood waiting.

And spontaneity? Completely lacking.
Do I dare? was a never-ending backing
To every song I ever longed to sing.
Well, now I've had enough. I'll do my thing
And never talk of Michelangelo
Again, thank god. He had to go.
That dreadful man was nothing but a leech.
Now I shall wear white linen trousers, and walk upon the beach.

Sunshine and equality

She preaches total equality, in business and the law,
In education, public loos, in bed, and on the floor
Of the Commons; she wants women running factories and farms,
But when the sun starts shining, she shaves under her arms.

History

I used to be quite definite about what's wrong and right;
I didn't live in dawn or dusk, knew only day and night;
But now the grey shades mean more, and I think before I speak.
This change, though common at my age, is historically unique –
I started as a Roman, but now I am a Greek.

Train in the distance

At night, with the wind in the right direction,
I could hear the hushed suggestion –
A chalk smudge in the air –
Of a whistle; I could swear
It, and dark doors opened, just a crack;
And sometimes the rails would sing;
But he – he never heard anything.
The train in the distance was only mine;
Even then it was merely single track,
But now it's an abandoned line.

Steam!
Once there was steam.
Once there was a dream
That we could conquer curves and ridges
With the gradients and the bridges
On a line that went for ever,
Where we'd never see the end,
No, we'd never see the end.

Now the trains that knifed the butter
Of the hills lie in the gutter
Of their graveyards, wrecked and rusty,
Seats and curtains oozing, musty,
And we won't see them again;
No, we won't see them again.

And the elemental powers
Fed from tenders and high water towers
Are silenced, tamed, and petrified,
Diseasled and electrified;
Quiet now, and cold;
Condemned for being old.

And the sight of pistons' passion
Has now fallen out of fashion;
The hum of loveless kissing
Drowns the sound of vapour hissing,
As new engines suck the arc of life from deadly shining rails,
For trains so indeterminate they can't tell heads from tails.

And theoristic economic deities rank higher
In the running of the railways than the old great god of fire;
But the tell-tale hairs still bristle at a misty distant whistle;
And we still see down the siding where our memories are hiding,
And we keep them fully stoked with the smell of burning smoke,
And we hear the *whoosh!* and feel the push
And taste the coal and know the soul –
We taste the coal and know the soul –
And again we have the dream
That we had when there was steam.

The company of poets

The company of poets has no mission statement,
Except, perhaps, for the singing of birds –
We don't waste words.
This company keeps no accounts.
Our work can't be measured in figures and amounts –
Our books are always unbalanced,
A loss increases our raw materials,
And we are our own prophets.
The company of poets is multinational.
The world is our concern
And we refuse to discern
Regional differences in lying power.
We do not clock in or out.
We have a deadline every hour,
Which we always miss,
And a lifeline in each kiss –
Fraternisation is encouraged.
Our workplace is untidy.
We have foraged
Through dustbins, on our way to the top,
Where we don't stop
Rummaging through rubbish,
Seeking the best letter in the litter.
The company of poets may be hungry and lean
But that does not mean
We are fitter
To survive against competition;
We attack from a weak position,
Always.
There are no personnel records.
Our days
Are not counted, and we are unnumbered.
For our success, we set no targets.
We are not encumbered
With policies, shareholders, or bored directors,
And we have no company cars.
We are driven by stars
And truth.
We have no lie detectors.

The company of poets has no community outreach.
We send the right message to many ears
And teach
As a way of facing our fears.
This company is public, but never limited.
No crime is committed
When we give away secrets;
We have no liabilities.
The company is sometimes measured by performance,
But an objective way of judging our abilities
Has not been found.
We have no peers, so there can be no jury.
The basis for the company of poets is not sound,
But perhaps it is; or perhaps it is fury.
The company of poets is always in the hands of the receivers,
Who invest the savings in hope,
Because they are believers
In tomorrow,
And we borrow heavily, but repay with interest.
We give a good return, of glimpses and surprises,
Affirmations, promises, love, wildness, rest;
The company of poets does not win any prizes,
But in today's marketplace,
It is the best,
For the company of poets looks after its own,
And gives all that it has;
We are never alone.
(It's also full of bitches,
Sad old farts and wicked witches,
But they don't belong in this poem.)

Justified

Just today I just noticed that I use the
word just just about all the time,
instead of only which makes me feel
lonely, and indecently often in place
of recently, and sometimes when I
really mean merely, or dearly, or,
queerly, even really itself; or, more
matter-of-factly, when I should put
exactly; and it certainly isn't prudery
that avoids the hint of rudery in
setting down, squarely, barely. I've
never denied despite my pride that I
can be idle, and don't always take the
trouble to decide the precise word for
my meaning, but sidle round with this
vague evasion; but it's annoying and
demeaning that the occasions are
strangely rare that I use just to signify
fair; where, in fact, it would be truly
justified.

Play school

When I am old, I shall wear purple;
A pleated skirt, with toning blouse
In lilac polyester.
And twice a week, with the other old cows,
I will not be allowed to fester
At home; I will visit the day centre,
Where a nice lady called Esther
From *Young at Arts*
Will teach me to make imitation stained glass
From tacky torn-up tissue,
Stuck with kiddies' glue;
The windows will be adorned with the resulting panes.
We will all clap.
And for months their loose edges will flap,
Annoying a kind lady called Jane,
Who will bring, from the museum,

Sweet wrappers from my youth,
To encourage reminiscence,
And alleviate the tedium.
And a kind lady whose name I will not remember
Will come from the library in November
To read us autumn poetry; no escape from Keats.
We will paint leaves on poem sheets.
And Christmas lunch will be served in December,
On or about the seventh,
And subsequently,
On the eleventh,
I will be exercised gently:
A kind lady from the NHS
Will get me tapping my feet
To rhythms relentlessly jolly.
We will make decorations with artificial holly.
And I will be coddled by Molly,
The helper; served coffee with much too much milk,
As I paint Japanese symbols on silk.
There will always be games there for me to play;
If arthritis allows I will do macramé,
And go on the day trip to Blackpool.

It will be just like play school   .
But I am already full grown.
How will I get them to leave me alone?

Committed
He failed, because he never really tried
To kill himself; was always found before he actually died.
He wasn't a committed suicide.

The knot

I woke up one morning with a small knot in my hair.
My lover offered to brush it out, but I rather liked it there.
It developed daily, and I treated it with care.

It's a knot, not nits, I noted. Having it untangled
Would have been like an abortion, or a new-born baby strangled.
He just thought I was twisted too, and my new attachment rankled.

Its complexities increased each day, its personality grew.
He said, *The knot, or me!* and I soon chose – *The knot, not you,*
And as he left, I drank champagne; I gave the knot shampoo.

We were intimate companions, shared a pillow every night,
But perhaps too close for comfort; she – the knot - wanted the right
To independence; and all too soon her teeth, like the comb's,
        began to bite.

And I too wanted freedom. *Get out of my hair!* I cried.
But with an angry snarl, *No, you get out of mine!* she replied,
But neither of us could quite shake loose; our bonds were tightly tied.

There would have to be a parting – I think that we both knew it,
But once you've woven a web, how on earth do you undo it?
Should I shave the whole lot off? Would it be better if I grew it?

I twirled and curled my problem; what should I do about it?
I was frightened, now, of being alone, couldn't think of life without it;
And could I really cut her off? Somehow I began to doubt it.

But there's always a solution; I'm not defined by what I wear,
Or the way that I look, or habits like biting my thumbs and
        twiddling my hair;
I'm not really anxious and mousy; there's a carefree blonde inside –
And the knot grew weaker and withered. It wasn't murdered –
        only dyed.

Stream of consciousness
or One step at a time
or Dream sequence
Bed.
Sleep.
Dream.
Scheme...
Plan!
Man.
Can,
Will!
Kill.
Pill?
Push?
Cushion?
Blow?
Dart?
Heart
Break.
Shaken!
Wake.
Taken,
Fucked.
Faked,
   again.
      Amen.

Your voice
Your voice speaks to me
Of places where I want to be,
Close and distant, sure, unknown; the sea
Waves in your modulations,
And the desert's undulations
Underlie your undertones,

And – your voice speaks to me
In every voice that isn't yours;
It sings to me up stairways,
And calls down corridors,
And I think I hear your whisper in the closing of lift doors;
And every stranger's sound
Brings brief belief that I have found
You, but they're only imitations
Of your soft sweet intonations;

'Cause – your voice speaks to me,
So I ring when you're not in,
Longing for your answerphone announcement to begin;
When you say *Sorry, I'm not here,*
But leave a message, loud and clear,
Then I'm sure you must mean me!

But – when your voice speaks, you see
I don't know what I want to say,
And I stay crumpled up and quiet;
And I don't know why it
Is this way,
And just as I did yesterday,
I promise that tomorrow
I will beg or steal or borrow
Words to tumble in a riot
Of bright colours in your mind
So you'll find what it's like to be
Bewildered, dazzled, dumbstruck, blinded:
As I know I'll be when –
Your voice speaks to me again.

Vanilla
You know, I am quite happy
With the colour of my skin -
Not quite pink, or beige, or white,
It's well-adapted to this northern light
Where I need to let the sun seep in.

I have no bitter quarrel
With the land where I was grown,
Where all the people whom I meet
Are free to carp, despise and moan.
If you dance to a different beat,
So what? I find your difference sweet -
You will not dance alone.

I will not take the blame
For all my great-grandparents' crimes.
My genes do not inherit guilt,
And their sins, their sins are not mine,
And my kids' future won't be built
On self-abasement's low designs.

Please, don't assume that you know me.
Don't brush me with vanilla tar.
I *love* your pride in who you are,
And I too claim my right to be.

Guitar quartet
Yours
Make me yours.
Caress my curves with calloused hands,
Stand holding me, enfolding me,
And I will open doors;
I own all keys.
You want a mistress or a whore,
A lover or a slave?
I'll be all these.
Stroke me soft, and I'll behave;
Pay me attention every day,
Mention me each time you pray,
Practise like a monk your art
And I will sing the sounds your heart
Can't say; together we can break all bounds
And bands and earthly laws
And slide away, where angels soar
And demons play.

Make me yours,
And I will hug you, I will drug you
Surer than the strongest spliff;
With every riff I'll make it plain
I'm your cocaine, your LSD,
Your E A D C B and E, again,
There is no bigger thrill than me!
So please, make me yours,

And strum me, pluck me,
Finger me – yes, fuck me
In a rhythm with no pause
Until dramatically, climactically,
The music pumps and pours,
Then share with me the crowd's applause –

And I'll be yours.

Mine

You useless lump of wire and wood!
I should have dumped you when I could,
But now you're underneath my skin,
Where nothing else has ever been –
I can't leave you alone;
I need you for my own.
But when you sing for him, your tone
Is sweeter than I ever made
You give me; I'm betrayed,
And now I hate the thing I played
With love; this millstone
Round my neck – you turn my fingers into clay,
And my sense tells me to say
Be free!
You're better off with him than me!
But my senses beg for one more day;
I can't give you away –
You're mine, and mine you'll stay.

Fuse

He doesn't sing.
Why should he, when his strings
Like cheesewire cut through words,
Stripe scars across my soul?

He is not whole.
His guitar gives him a voice.
And when he wants to speak to me
There isn't any choice to choose;
He is compelled to fuse with wood
And steel and electricity,
And turn the volume right up loud
To reach me through misguided crowds
Who all think they're the one
For whom the music has begun;

But when the gig is over,
The guitar's back on its stand,
The plectrum's in his pocket –
He'll reach out for my hand,
And stare at me in silence,
And know I understand.

Metaphor
There's no point writing poems, for
It's sure as eggs is eggs:
The guitarist grips a metaphor,
Pointing up between his legs.

Black guitar
My black guitar
plays minor chords –
music's sad swords
slice songs of love,
tragically
unrequited.
I want to be
a major key –
happy tunes may
be clichéd, but
that's what I'd like
now. And always.
This skill seems quite
beyond me, though.

Perhaps one day,
who knows, these dark
inversions will
be righted, and
the songs I sing
grow bright; as if
my guitar might
magically
change colour and
turn white.

I just saw a guitar floating down the Thames
You played that song for her,
And now you'll never play again!
And she picked up his guitar,
And she flung it in the Thames.
Now it was drifting past me,
A sad and dirty swan,
With a neck held low in shame,
Playing only river songs.

We need a few more shots!
Please just lean backwards; rock and roll!
The guitar slipped away for a soggy stroll;
An escape from Jack and Coke -
It never minded the odd toke,
But it was worried for its sanity,
And now it sought serenity:
The life of a slow boat;
And it was happy just to float.

You mean nothing but frustration!
I can't play you - so damnation!
And he dropped it overboard,
With one last weed-infested chord
That sounded sweet as icy springs.
He had made the guitar sing,
But oh! Too late! The echo faded,
And the guitar - well, it couldn't swim;
Couldn't breaststroke back to him.
Aah! It gently weeps, he said,
But he had made the watery bed
In which it sailed; he'd failed;
And the guitar was laughing to be free,
No strings attached, and heading for the sea.

Your time has come, my sweetest friend.
Her tears soaked into varnish,
Yellow, wrinkled with old age.
Your score has reached its final page.
Sleep sound; let waters take you.
I can't let any stranger break you.
With the tiniest of pushes,
She cast it from the shore,
The guitar that needed rest;
The guitar that she would play no more.

I just saw a guitar, acoustic,
Floating down the Thames,
Playing its lonely game of Poohsticks.
Why? Where from? I'll never know
What tunes it hums as it sinks below,
In a damp diminuendo, after the Embankment's bend.
I watch the mainstream take it to the bridge,
And silently applaud as its rippling music ♪♪♪ ends.

Picked
Picture this.
Picture this moment;
On a playing field that has always been unlevel,
A selection committee, consisting of
All the people you ever fouled,
Or cornered,
Consult a record of red cards,
Lines crossed, offsides;
And consider penalties.
And before you go for the free kicks,
Remember that one day,
They
Will be picking teams.

For remembrance
Buy a poppy for remembrance?
The old soldier said to me,
With, it seemed, no awareness
Of the bloody irony
That, before it was disturbed by war,
The bareness of Afghanistan saw
Field on field of red –
A crop grown just for cash,
Which, more than alcohol or hash,
Helped westerners forget.

Scarlet springs in streets there now;
The harvest hasn't finished yet.

M:W > 1
How do you know if you've written a poem?
There are clues that give it away.
It might have rhyme or rhythm;
New-ploughed imagery, no old cliché;
It may have a form or a structure –
Perhaps haiku, or rondeau redoublé;
But the best, most reliable measure
Lies in how much each syllable can say.
There's even a formula to show how it's done –
The ratio of meaning to words must be greater than one.

Duty
My mum told me it was my duty
To suffer for the sake of beauty;
She thought the only way to please a
Man was with the aid of tweezers.
When I refused eyebrow extraction,
She warned I'd get no satisfaction;
But despite my ducking all her plucking,
I've suffered from no lack of
            friends of the opposite sex.

Waiting

I cannot move, I cannot walk;
There's no-one here – can't even talk;
My book's too far away to reach;
It's not as if I'm on a beach,
As timeless as a pearly shell,
Just watching as the clouds float by;
I'm sitting here as bored as hell,
Waiting for my nails to dry.

Henley

They arrive so smoothly, gently –
In the Rolls or in the Bentley;
The women are so lady-like,
The men so gentlemenly.
They line up at the entry;
Wait for tickets so patiently,
Until I, quite accidentally,
Join the queue, not at the end. The
Swift rebuke is cold, unfriendly:
"I say, we don't push in, in Henley."

Beauty is truth

Some people swear by cannabis, cocaine or ecstasy;
But give me gadgets and inventions, electronic circuitry;
I flick a switch for trips and kicks – I get high on LCD;
If I want mind expansion, liquid crystals do it for me!

Although my passion's poetry, I'm turned on by technology,
I feel the fizz in physics, find karma in pharmacology,
I make merry with mathematics, I'm brightened by biology,
And I see no contradiction in this unified psychology,

For just as maths and music have a harmony that's shown.
It is clear that even scientists can't live by head alone,
And they share a soul with poets with a link that should be known,
Though communication's difficult – poets are frightened by the phone.

But a poet must ask questions, and that's what researchers do;
They're all trying to seek out whatever's beautiful and true,
And there's perfection in a formula, as well as in haiku;
Precision in a mystery, as Albert Einstein knew.

Though what we'll know tomorrow is a secret not yet shared,
Often scientists and poets are the only ones who've cared
To work on what makes life worth living; only a dreamer
        could have dared
To see the magic in a line like e=mc².

And there's other things in common – we all have lots of fun:
Our endeavours have results that are undreamt when just begun;
And there is a common formula to tell how it is done:
The ratio of meaning to words must be greater than one.

And some truisms are really true – like *well, it takes all kinds,*
But with poetry and science there can be meeting of minds.
For poets see eternal truths, when they look between the lines,
And scientists make poems, though, unlike me, they don't use rhymes.

And four cruel laws affect us all, which it seems must be obeyed:
1. No-one listens to us – it's as if they are afraid;
2. Our reputations are short-lived, and very quickly fade;
3. We're all too busy working to spend much time getting laid;
4. Both scientists and poets are undervalued and underpaid.

Hairdon't
I try to make it obey my will,
But my unruly hair just won't.
I comb, and curse, and curl, but still
End up with a hairdon't.

Weather forecast
We need to talk now
Means always a storm of words
Before silence rains.

Covers
How's that? I say, presenting him with flannels, freshly-pressed.
I love to see him dressed like this;
The clover's kiss
Of cream against the green;
So clean.
It's the washing-line appeal;
The feel, again,
Of innocence, of boys' games played by men.
No muddy shorts, no dirty thoughts intrude
To spoil the sporting mood
Or smear this spotless day.

But when the game is over, it will be our turn to play.
And if they triumph in the match
He will be my winning catch,
Because, underneath the covers,
Proud cricketers make perfect lovers.

Don't sleep with me
They should give you a warning.
They should be forced, by law,
To wear a placard round their necks:
Don't sleep with me – I snore.

To my grown-up children: Advice at Christmas from me, your mother,
who as you know never gives advice unless asked, even though she - I
- always knows best.
One. Christmas is not a test.
If your presents are not perfect,
This does not mean your partner loves you less
Than you love him stroke her;
Please don't infer that passion's gone;
It's merely that you're better at using Amazon.

Two. Please feel free.
I don't want you to think that you should come home to me.
I'd much rather you were where you want to be.

But three, please *do* send me a card.
Preferably one that's funny.

Though, four - don't spend too much money
On what is in fact a worthless decoration.
I don't need fifteen pounds' worth
Of cardboard adoration.

Five. Don't eat meat that's still alive.
Salmonella threats are true;
Make sure your turkey's cooked right through.
And for God's sake, don't use frozen roasties,
Not after the last time.
For me, a slice of scrambled eggs on toast is quite enough.

Six. Please don't give me stuff
That will just hang around the house collecting dust.
A bunch of flowers, if you must;
A chosen book, a loving look,
An unexpected visit would be better.
And in return for my gifts, perhaps a letter?
Email? Phone call?
Text, with smily face?

Seven. Your place is with *your* families now.
Please trust me when I say I'm fine alone.
As you know, I was accustomed to being on my own,
Which brings me to the big one…

Eight. Please, please don't do what I did.
Don't ever leave *your* kids,
Because Christmas Day for me meant taking round your presents,
Being thanked politely, and dismissed;
Not hugged or kissed;
Returning to a house that begged for laughter,
With no thought of happy-ever-after -
Just guilt, regrets and tears,
A tapestry of sorrow I stitched alone for years,
With just a muttered prayer to God-knows-who, that
        things might change.
Remember, life *is* strange,
And he - she - it moves in mysterious ways.
However bad things seem right now, there will be better days,
Just as, at last, my Christmas dreams came true.
And I was back with you.
There was new birth that warm, transformed December.
We played Trivial Pursuit, as I remember,
After lunch. I lost the game,
But all the same, I won everything. No doubt.

Nine. Never forget what this is all about.
We have no religion, you and I;
We don't see magic stars up in the sky,
But every Christmas, for angels (like you) and men
(Which includes me),
Hope *is* born again.

Ten. For everything that you receive, give thanks -
Even if it's just socks or pants,
Or smiles; or love;
Or kindness; or forgiveness,
For which I now thank you.

Eleven. Kindly disregard all of the above.
Who am I to give advice?
All I can do is send my love,
Although to see you would be nice.
If you feel like it, get in your cars and come.

But just have a happy Christmas, kids,
With all my love, your Mum.

Alchemy

The creepers' leaves are oxidised –
Though I don't understand what lies
Behind their acid's burn to rust –
And fallen; but when all else dies,
The naked stem, like me, relies
On an alchemy of hope and trust.

A&E

There's not much poetry here,
Just polished floors seen from a wheelchair,
And the hurt cries of a child,
And some lonely, broken people,
And my feelings of self-pity.

There's not much poetry here,
Just the polished moves of comfort
As a nurse applies the plaster,
And the cool hands of a doctor
That can soothe a small girl's whimpers,
And the relatives on white chargers
Who bring smiles to patients' faces –
The security of care,
Not diminished by the numbers.

I felt I was a person,
Not a subject or a papertrail;
Not just fall - fracture - female,
As they wiped away my tears.
So who needs poetry here?

Knot yet

Today I found it, in a jacket pocket:
A slightly stained blue hankie, knotted
At one corner. Yours;
Left to remind me, like the hair strand in my locket,
As if I could forget; a spotted
Forget-me-knot, I thought, and smiled,
Beguiled with my surprised discovery.
What the knot was for,
I don't know now, of course.
I should have made a note.
But I'm guessing that not crying at reminders
Means my journey to recovery
Is progressing. Still. It's time to wash the coat,
Throw out the bits of fluff,
Old lists, and tickets – all that lot;
But as yet I think that that's enough;
The hankie will stay stained;
And I won't untie the knot.

Tomato

No tomato bursting from its skin could be more red than you;
No floppy faithful Labrador more reliable or true;
No screaming warplane slicing skies could give more sense of power.
Your classic lines eclipse the grace of any well-bred flower;
No cashmere coat compares against the comfort that you give.
You turn on my ignition and rev up my will to live.
In fact, I just could not be fonder
Of anything than my Honda.

Orion's belt

Of all the constellations,
There's only one I know:
Orion's belt. They call it that,
But really it's just three stars in a row.

Veil of tears

I dress
Not to please, or to impress,
But to express.
Every sweater is a herald,
Every pair of jeans professes
My persona for the day.
Even my knickers know their place –
Strong and steely grey,
Or of the prettiest pink lace –
They echo silently the feelings featured on my face.

But I have never worn a veil.
I don't feel the need to hide
Or to conceal under this modern-day chain mail.
The unspoken implication would be:
I'd set out to fail,
To fake, or break communication;
That I could no longer trust
The people I might meet,
And that the fire of future friendship
Was just dust beneath our feet.

I couldn't rot under this pall,
This deathbed caul;
I'm not in thrall to god or any man,
Who will tell me what I can
Or cannot do.
And there's one thing that I'm sure is true:
If I had a god, a supreme being,
All-knowing and all-seeing,
Then he would not be ashamed of me,
And I would not be blamed
Because of things that other people see.
And when I am confronted by a living shroud,
It is for me a vale of tears,
Although, it appears, I'm not allowed
To say so.
I'm saddened, because I cannot be your friend.
Our relationship's at an end
Before it's started; our ways parted

Before we've even met,
Because this barrier won't let me forget
That my open faith in you has been rejected.
It isn't you, but me; I'm not accepted,
Tolerated; *my* beliefs are underrated,
By this cloth
Which might as well be jet;
While my clothes smile hello,
Yours say *keep off.*

And yet, and yet –
Freedom is the only god I follow.
So I swallow my distaste, my hurt,
And, putting on my rainbow shirt
I say, *Why shouldn't they*
Dress any way they think is right?
Let them be smothered
Up in darkness,
Symbolise perpetual night!
But I can't just not be bothered.
I'm not heartless,
And I still think what a waste
It is for beauty to be covered,
Not a chance of an unruly glance,
A frown, a smile, a kiss!
For the essence of my humanism is this:
No-one should need a mask, or a disguise,
Because if there is a god worthy of worship,
Then all of us are beautiful in his eyes.

Not a word
I used to look with pity
At the couples sitting
Silently, with not a word
To say.
But now I have a man;
I understand how silence can
Be better than the non-stop drivel I have heard
Today.

One thing

My dear, I'd cut my hair for you,
My hair so long and fine;
I'd choose what clothes to wear for you –
You can take that as a sign;
I'd write poems in a book for you –
Nine hundred and ninety-nine!
I'd even try to cook for you
(If you brought *lots* of wine).
I'd do all this and more
If I were sure that you'd be mine –
But, please, don't ever ask me
To wax my bikini line.

Class act, or
When you go into a school as a visiting writer, the kids are...

Not quite dominoes. Not quite blank,
Each slate equipped with regulation blobs –
Eyes, mouth, and nose; and education
Being as it is, they're not in rows,
But sat round tables, armoured
In innocence; blameless, battle-ready visors
Blanketing their faces. To me, they're nameless.
I know them only by the places where they sit,
These people undefined by time,
Waiting to be knocked down
By my bland promises.

Whistling woman

It said I shouldn't whistle
In the paper's beauty page –
It would accentuate my wrinkles,
And emphasize my age;
Huh! Shows that they nothing
Of one of life's more pleasant truths –
That even old cool chicks who whistle
Never wrinkle; they just groove.

Missed midnight

It isn't just another day,
But each morning's new awareness
Multiplied three hundred times,
And, added in, a bookcase full of journals
Whose first pages show blank lines –
Unwritten dedications
To loneliness, despair,
Presentiments of death, and numb betrayal.
But I buy hope in every New Year sale
From revellers shouting greetings in the street,
And get drunk on vinegar bubbles
Of expectation that this year will bring treats
In place of troubles.

Last night was not dramatic;
No fireworks smashed our skies;
But neither was it treacherous nor traumatic;
There was no dying dance or starlit lies,
And this year I will write:
I went to meet my lover, watched a film, missed midnight;
And no matter what you say,
For me, it isn't just another day.

PowerPoint

Hooray for the PowerPoint moment
When slides slip,
Technology trips up,
And only words and people still remain.
It is no loss. We gain
From listening, from looking
At expressions on the speakers' faces,
Rather than blank spaces on a screen.
Empty phrases where the bullet points have been.
Tell us the story, leave PowerPoint behind –
You are all we need to fill our minds.

Clinging

Let us consider Blu Tack.
It clings, without complaint, to any surface.
Its sole purpose in life is to adhere.
It moulds to fit new contours,
Contentedly accepts each change of shape
And way of life.
Lacking personality, or any self-esteem,
It adapts with ease;
Adopts, with just the slightest strain or squeeze,
Another's features,
Habits, loves and hates, and manners.
And then it is ignored, for years,
And all remaining life within it
Slowly leaches out like tears
In air; it cracks
And crumbles, dries and changes tack,
Seeks freedom in a new direction –
A suicidal insurrection –
It pulls itself away, but unsupported, falls and dies,
And is trodden into pieces where it lies.

For Ruth

The first night that I slept there,
In the corner of an orchard,
In a caravan with thin tin walls,
The calls of ewes, lambs taken,
Filled the stillness of the night with cries,
Till moonfall.
I didn't think they'd care,
And, sure enough, the next night
All was peaceful.

But for my friend, whose teenage son is missing –
Shorn and shivering in the cold light
Of the Christmas streets and New Year dawn –
Missing; presumed; the rest is left unsaid –
For her the moon will never set;
Love's noisy stars will never go to bed.

211

Seduction

It's half-past midnight,
And I am half-past fifty,
And though a bit less nifty than
Once I might have been,
Still, at around twelve-thirty
I start feeling very flirty
Towards my bed.
Look at it.
It's so-o-o-o-o horizontal.
It beckons with full-frontal frankness –
Lay your body down on mine!
At noon its tempter's task is thankless,
I barely even cast a glance,
But now – oh, wouldn't it be fine,
If I had only half a chance,
To turn my axis upside down,
Parallel the unforgiving ground,
Put closed signs down over my face –
My eyelids in their *proper* place –
And, following them, let back and bum
Come to accept its warm embrace,
The seduction of the quilt.
Oh, to give in, feel no guilt –
I confess, I am quite smitten.
But there are still things to be done:
I've got to get this fucking poem written.

When love goes...

...it never really goes, you said.
Almost a watermark on thin paper;
less impressive than a footprint;
less tangible than dust motes;
more like homeopathy.
But there is no evidence for
the millionth dilution.
I don't believe in alternative medicine,
and neither do you,
really.

To the Queen
"Normal BBC language rules apply."
The ink on the letter was barely dry
Before I'd called them on the phone,
To say my piece – my whinge, my moan
About censorship. "Well, we must take care,"
The producer said, "for on radio, there
"Is no late-night watershed, you see.
"To tell you the truth, between you and me,
"It's a dreadful faff to get *anything* through.
"The f-word means a tremendous to-do:
"The Controller has to be asked to approve;
"I have to justify it, to prove
"It's essential. I do hope you see what I mean."
She paused. "And, please, don't use anything worse
"In your – what is it called? – slam poetry verse,
"Because – cunts have to go to the Queen!"

Always one
There's always one.
We've all been caught, she says,
Laughing all over her lime-green coat.
It's the wrong note to play.
The rest of us say nothing,
Waiting for our cues
In silence, here to pay our dues
For breaking limits,
Driving at too fast a speed.
The coffee's free, but there's nothing here to read.
Perhaps enforced reflection on our misdeeds
Is part of the course,
Par for the course on speed awareness.
A moment's lapse: a cup of tea is spilled.
She in the green is clearly careless;
The rest of us more sombre.
Yet how many among our number
Truly repent, and think:
I might have killed?

Halfway down the stairs
I remember this.
It's how I felt when I was eight,
Arriving home, my mother late –
No sign of her downstairs,
Or up.
Abandoned.
My cup of cares was hard to hold,
And halfway down it overflowed,
And I would sit and cry,
And wonder why
She'd gone.

Things haven't changed.
Don't think it strange
That it's stairs I choose to sit upon
Now you say that you're leaving.
It never stops, the grieving.

Yes, I remember this,
But then, it was made better
By a kiss.

Condemned
It's just a box for living in –
Four walls, a roof, a floor.
But it was more, much more
Than this. How many lives,
Each one a miracle, spooled
Their foolish loves and times
Of wisdom in this place?
How many faces gazed
Through these small windows?
How many spells of love were cast,
How many tangled curses?
How many tears of death
And birth flowed through from door to door?
Magic flashed here; but no more.
It is condemned.

Box camera
Cut down a whippy sapling
While it shivers in a coastal breeze,
And slice it into silver sticks,
And take the wax that honey bees
Leave over, and my box is made.

It shows a film that will not fade;
All the bits I don't want back:
The angry plates at dinner-time;
The girl with glasses standing by
While netball teams are picked and chosen;
The football match spectator, frozen,
There because of just one boy;
The London flat where all weekend
She spoke to no-one; the best friend
Who was, always, the pretty one;
The furious kicking of her son,
Abandoned; and the scrambled egg
For Christmas dinner, left uneaten;
The brave competitor, beaten.
The last breaths. The deaths.

Bury the box, away from the sun.
Let the film run, and run, and run.

Anagram
There's no play any more;
No need to bother with the fore.
Sitting up in bed,
She flicks through a magazine;
He has the paper, folded.
Soon, they will turn out the light.
"Anagram of bedroom?"
Hangs in the air,
Before they say goodnight.

Lullaby seat
It rocks,
my swing seat,
with the gentle beat
of bouncing prams
and mother's arms –
the cradle that I never had,
but craved.

I bought it in a sale –
the Co-op, twenty quid;
best thing that I ever did.
It is my Prozac when I'm sad;
a fairground ride, but well-behaved;
its comforts never fail.
It keeps me sane.
It doesn't even mind the rain
as it gentles me from heel to toe.
It is the place I always go
when I want to be a child again.

The price of love
They all start out shiny,
Full of promise; well-defined –
The pattern sharply etched, the lines
Cut deep around the rim.
I take one from my pocket,
Newly-minted, and it's him.
I keep it for a little while
Alone, apart, beside my bed,
As if it's something special,
But one day, it isn't there.
I haven't cared enough.
Instead of treasure it's just money,
Mixed in with all the other coins,
In a purse that's full of stories.

Each apostrophe
Misplaced in *its* equals a
Stroke in Tunbridge Wells.

If you count each foot
To make a perfect poem,
Is this podantry?

Flippy

Fur fell in my house. A selective snow
That covered cushions, people, throws;
A fine brown down, the moultings of a duckling
Unhardened yet by winter.

But this was far from baby fluff.
Flippy, old, but still as soft as stuff
That dreams are made on, gave us
Insulation with good grace,
Shedding drifts around the place
As if she didn't care
About her hair.

The furniture is cleaner now;
Clothes are bald again,
Defurred. I remember when
I met her thistledown with a curse.
But Flippy's absence is much worse.

Prelude

You were my work of art,
and much more useful
than a Degas or Picasso,
and much cheaper.
My dad would have been pleased
that a bequest from him
allowed me to become
your registered keeper,
because he had a Mini Cooper S.
I've been fond of other cars,
but my feelings for you are
more complex; stronger, deeper –
I love you now no less
than on the day we met.
I will not forget
your shape, style, speed and grace,
and especially your dashboard
and the view of you from the front
which looks just like a smiling face.
You were the best.
But now, my friend, it's time for you
to have a well-earned rest.
And I would like to think
that you were going to meet your maker,
but the truth is, it's betrayal,
and you're headed for the breakers.

With fishes

I would like to swim with fishes –
My superpower –
Not reading minds or bending spoons
Or flying, one arm stretched in front,
To rescue people trapped in fiery buildings.
No.
I would like to swim with fishes,
Naked, free of scales.
Not around these shores, of course;
In some warm seas
Where Greeks met Persians,
That's where I would like to swim with fishes,
Breathing brine, no tubes or tanks required.
Through this I would escape
From people talking;
People dressed in clothes that I could never wear
And still look human.
The sea would be my scarf,
The waves my haircut,
And my steady stream of bubbles
Would not reach
The edge of the page,
Or the beach.

Yet

I want to fall in love again!
But, frankly, lust would do.
I want to need to take my pen
And write about a new man who
Stirs my viscera like custard,
Makes my senses sharp as mustard,
Has that same effect as one last cigarette,
Helps me abandon, escape, forget,
And ideally pays off all my debt!
But I haven't met him yet.

Some days

Some days, edges are sharp,
weeds picked out in ballast,
clear as hilltop trees in a dying sun.
Still lifes of stones on sleepers
await a painter's eye;
the fretwork awning razored,
laundry-white; and dry-cleaned
business people match suits.

But today, the track is stained
with train droppings;
The people dull and ill-attired,
put together by a careless boy.
The birds can't get their act together:
one-note shotguns,
they attack the air with no rhythm.
Today, no children are warned
away from the blunt edge,
but they probably should be.

Dancing with my mum

Last time I took you off
For a weekend in a hotel
That the brochure boasted, quietly,
Was reserved for "adults only",
Which, as I soon discovered,
Had no naughty implications,
Just a carvery of age;
Last time I brought you here,
You were goaded into dancing
By a birthday girl of ninety,
Who sashayed past our seats.
If she can, so can I, you said,
And hauled me to the dance floor.
We jigged around our handbags
Like two teenagers, half-speed.

This time, you brought a stick.
It lay resting on the chair back,
Not really up to waltzing,
Let alone the jive or twist.
You sat and watched the dancers,
And I wished that we could join them;
I wished that you would join them,
But you are not ninety, yet.

The man who
Look at him, the arrogant sod -
He struts around like he was God.
He's sleekly groomed and deckshoe shod -
He's everything we're not.

He expects us plebs to let him pass;
He treats us as his private farce;
He's got his head stuck up his... stern.
Do we like him? We do not.

He does what he wants to do.
He likes to down a drink or two.
Splice the mainbrace! Here's to you!
In truth, a drunken sot...

Who likes to mix with those who sail,
Though you'd never catch him trying to bail.
He thinks he is an alpha male,
He can't even tie a knot.

He is the shark without a fin;
The lamprey sucking on our skin -
He screws us while he wears a grin,
And he doesn't care a jot.

He is the man we love to hate.
We hope one day he'll meet his fate.
Is he some mighty head of state?
No - just a man who owns a yacht.

Fire and ice
Don't give me a diamond;
Forget the Maserati;
You can keep your Cotswold mansion
And the champagne-swilling party.
I don't need crack or heroin;
No frocks from posh designers;
No truffles and no caviar -
For me there's nothing finer
        than
                words.

I can use my pencil's carbon
As a rocket squibbing light;
Turn penstrokes into ecstasy;
And with the words I write
I'll put diamonds in your eyes
And an ocean in your ears -
I will house you in a palace,
Drive you faster than your fears.

I'll get you drunk on imagery,
And stuff you full of lies;
I'm a pusher with a poem;
A magician in disguise.
I'll dress you like an emperor
In robes of velvet passion.
Reality is anything
My craftsman's mind can fashion.

So why should I want diamonds?
I have my private mine,
And I'll work to cut and polish
Every facet, every line,
And I'll give them to you freely
Till you drown in fire and ice,
And the only thing I crave
Is your accolade: "That's nice!"

Too many

I have too many chairs;
Too many clothes, and no-one to wear
Them for; my bed is much too wide;
My table has too many sides.
I have too many mugs and plates,
Let alone knives; and of late
I feel I've had too many lives.
Too many pens; no-one to send
My letters to. Too many things to do,
And none that really matters.
Too many tatters of memory,
Hanging from too many days;
And it isn't over yet.
I have too many ways not to forget.

Hatched, matched, detached, re-attached, despatched
Dive in

Dive in.
Dive in; give in; live in this;
This origin of everything,
This ultimate of unions,
This Mediterranean of marriage.
Wallow in its warmth,
Frolic in its freedom,
Be supported,
As the salt of unconditional commitment
Causes tears to disappear,
Calms storms;
Cleanses wounds and clears old fears.

Cast off the clothes of caution,
And with nothing but a ring to keep you buoyant,
Trust your senses and dive in,
And swim – vulnerable, together –
In a never-ending sea of limitless love.

Close the book
Just close the book.
This particular story's at an end.
It opened well, with promises and fire;
You thought you'd found a character you could love;
A special friend; an object of desire;
But, somehow, the plot went wrong.
Perhaps it lingered on too long;
Perhaps a sequel beckoned,
Or telling tales turned into lies;
Perhaps no reason can be reckoned,
No finger put on why
Or how.
Perhaps it's left a bitter taste,
But at least it's over now;
And though you know you won't forget,
No story lived through is a waste,
And resolution needn't mean regret.

Twice
Some people jump from aeroplanes
Or hurtle on a bungee rope;
Some people disregard the risks
Of being president or Pope;
Some people find they can't say no,
And never wonder if they'll cope;
But nothing takes more confidence,
Endurance, courage, hope,
Than going against all good advice
And getting married twice.

Rubble
It's like climbing on loose scree.
We reach out for a twisted tree
Or scrabble for some rooted rock.
But what seemed an ordered stock of words
Is less secure than rubble,
And lips scrape on the gravel of cliché.

What is there to say?
Even mountains pass away,
Leaving no more trace
Than the memory of a face,
And though nothing seems more solid
Than this aching empty space,
We fumble to find comfort in a phrase of shifting sand,
And stumble towards a landscape we might one day understand.

Edgeways
We're called, sometimes, *les marginales;*
Loitering with intensity
On life's sidelines;
Showing a propensity
To be excused from games,
While longing for our names
To hit the headlines;
With a cynical belief
And a hopeless love of living,
Every one of us a thief
Who can't stop himself from giving –
We see things through a word-hedged haze,
A shifty look, an unpledged gaze;
Uncommitted; unadmitted;
                              edgeways.

Fuck off, poet
They come into my writing groups
And say, *I'm not creative, me.*
Can't make things up, can't draw,
Can't play; can't see what you lot see.

And I tell them – *That's bollocks.*
Give a two-year-old a paintbox -
He turns into Jackson Pollock,
Or a three-year-old a keyboard,
And she'll turn out tunes to make Beethoven cry.
(And her parents, too, probably).
Give a four-year-old a playmate
And together they'll beat Shakespeare.
They don't know they are creative;
They don't even have to try.

And there's always this reply:
Yeah, but it's knocked out of you at school, innit?
And I say: *Have you never played the fool?*
Have you never told a lie,
Or cover up some sad mistake?
Have you never taken photos,
Sung a song or baked a cake,
Danced along to cheesy music,
Like your dad, in some strange spasm;
Have you never faked an orgasm?
(Actually I don't really ask that; it would probably be considered
inappropriate.)
Made a baby?

And they say, *Maybe. But that's not poetry, is it?*
So I ask, *What would poetry be, then, if it were a thing?*
And they say:
A brand new pair of trainers;
Soft spring rain as it starts falling;
Vixens calling in the night;
A book with cold white empty pages;
Stepping stones across a river;

It is tigers kept in cages,
Or a wand with magic powers;
The sharp shock of a cold shower;
Wilting flowers given water;
It's a Man United shirt, and I'm an Arsenal supporter.
It's the first drive in a brand new car;
First coffee from a brand new jar;
The first cigarette after sex!
And being dumped by text.
It's having money in the bank,
Or just a solitary wank.
It's a brook that babbles on and on,
And on and on and on and on;
And - what's left when words are gone;
And (they say) *it's got to rhyme.*

This miracle happens every time.
And I read out what they've said,
And I say, *There! You're on your way.*
And they say, *Is that all it is then?*
I sigh:
Ever since man's been alive,
This has been key to our survival -
Your brain spends most of every day
Devising new and better ways of joining ends together -
You thought up gods who've made the weather,
And listened to the breezes bend the ears of wild grass -
Are they telling you it's prey, or could you be a lion's dinner?
It's been in yer from the start;
It's in your heart; it is your life,
To see a flint and think - a knife!
To turn a log into a wheel,
To find the herbs and words that heal;
And beat a rhythm that can wake the distant stars!
You don't learn to be creative - it's in everything you do.
And poetry brings sense when life's a farce.

And they look at me as if I'm a complete arse,
And one of them will say,
*Right then - if all that's true, we don't need **you**!*
So - fuck off, poet.

227

Index

109	20	*Counting seconds*	106
6th Street, Austin	156	*Covers*	202
A chair	153	*Cox*	39
A&E	205	*Cross-expressing*	36
Accents	159	*Cut*	21
Accident	144	*Damaged goods*	62
ADHD	120	*Damped*	151
Advice at Christmas	203	*Dancing with my mum*	220
Airport, Terminal 1	158	*Dangerous sports*	145
Alchemy	205	*Dive in*	223
Always one	213	*Dolphins*	34
Anagram	215	*Don't*	113
Assault	42	*Don't go out tonight*	131
Back	130	*Don't sleep with me*	202
Beauty is truth	200	*Dream seeds*	95
Beetling	180	*Dubya*	70
Beggars	125	*Duty*	199
Bert and me	58	*Dying men*	99
Betrayed	129	*Easy prey*	166
Black guitar	196	*Edgeways*	225
Boulder	129	*Entropy*	166
Box camera	215	*Epithalamion*	101
Bunches	8	*Except me*	113
Car park	133	*Fall from Grace*	92
Carbon footprint	84	*Ferry*	144
Cat bite	32	*Fiery Jack*	46
Cats' eyes	143	*Fire and ice*	222
Cell	114	*First kiss*	135
Cheek	160	*First reactions*	96
Class act	209	*First visit*	124
Clean	159	*Flagship*	6
Cliff face	158	*Flippy*	217
Clinging	211	*Folding time*	152
Close the book	224	*For remembrance*	199
Clownfish	95	*For Ruth*	211
COCABOG	68	*Free radicals*	73
Comfort zone	16	*Frog princess*	51
Committed	189	*Fuse*	195
Condemned	214	*Games*	64
Conundrum	169	*Gap*	151

Gates of fire 175
George Clooney 40
Glad rags 72
Gloucester prison 116
Gods 47
Gone now 132
Goodnight 94
Haiku written in prison 118
Hairdon't 201
Halfway down the stairs 214
Handbagged 54
Happy Hoover 49
Have you been? 56
Henley 200
Hero 79
History 184
Honey summers 26
Hope... 13
How do I love you? 180
How long? 138
I am a happy man 110
I don't want to write 153
I just saw a guitar 197
I know he hears 102
I will forget you 107
I'm suffering from stress 25
If I were... 126
If you wish to part 136
Imaginary 11
In praise of men 77
In the Greek way 172
In the snow 97
Indifference 179
Intelligent design 169
It's not like this in the movies 102
It's time I changed the bed 104
Just for me 163
Justified 188
Kefalonian vistas 170
Kilimanjaro 174

Kitten 160
Knot yet 206
La petite mort 149
La petite mort (2) 147
Lame 16
Land of the dead 104
Last night she hugged me 154
Light work 21
Like Everest, really 139
Like you 112
Losing your wings 98
Low flying 8
Lullaby seat 216
M:W > 1 199
Metaphor 196
Miaow 91
Mind the gap 37
Mine 195
Missed midnight 210
More 141
Mucky swans 181
My Achilles 142
My dog misses you 137
My masculine side 90
My octopus bed 168
My offering 165
NCP 127
Never Prufrock 183
Not a word 208
Not in charge 145
Not Reading 119
Not required 174
Nothing on 163
Nuts 81
Off and on 111
On falling in love 95
On nights like these 162
On platform 2 10
One thing 209
Only visiting 18
Orion's belt 206

Performance 22
Photograph 173
Picked 198
Plastic explosive 165
Play school 188
Playa del Ingles 65
Pockets 147
Poem or list? 29
Power 78
PowerPoint 210
Prelude 218
Prison education admin office
117
Prometheus 140
Pruning 24
Rainbows 128
Ramble 161
Rather drink 60
Reciprocity 135
Red daffodils 142
Rehearsal 9
Requiem 105
Robot 66
Routine measure 23
Rubble 225
SBB 10
Scars 17
Sea shelves 161
Seagulls 28
Seduction 212
See any Post House foyer 30
Sensible 146
Shamed 178
Shocked and surprised 176
Slam dunk 52
Sleep now 145
Sleeping 146
Sleeplessness 33
Socks 132
Solitary 24
Some days 220

Something of Greece 164
Somewhere to love 140
Soulsucker 15
Sounds of science 88
Starbucks 59
Steam! 185
Stream of consciousness 191
Substitute 76
Suicidal? 107
Sunshine and equality 184
Survival of the fruitiest 75
Swan 108
Talent 14
Ten different kinds of nothing
167
Tendernitis 106
Than this 86
The anarchist manifesto 12
The arbitrariness of edges 5
The company of poets 186
The effects of a Mediterranean
climate 169
The knack 150
The knot 190
The last song 109
The man who 221
The poem I would want to
read 12
The price of love 216
The same snow 115
Then 179
This man is innocent 123
This old house 18
This poem is repetitive 100
Three teabags and a plastic
soldier 117
Tidy 106
Tightrope 152
Time to go 171
To the Queen 213
Tomato 206

Tongues first	137	*Weather forecast*	201
Tonight	134	*Well, it's a start...*	177
Too many	223	*Weymouth*	175
Tower Bridge	148	*When a butterfly lands*	168
Train in the distance	184	*When ice caps melt*	7
Trapeze	150	*When love goes...*	212
Twice	224	*Where are you now?*	103
Universal metaphysics	27	*Where edges meet*	125
V for vanilla	44	*Whistling woman*	209
Vanilla	193	*Wireless*	172
Veil of tears	207	*Witchcraft on his lips*	82
Victims	116	*With fishes*	219
Victoria coach station, 5 a.m.		*Working for a living*	31
	157	*Written white*	27
Village idiot	168	*Yet*	219
Waiting	200	*Young offenders*	111
Washing	154	*Your voice*	192
Wave goodbye	162	*Yours*	194
We did	182		

#0065 - 220916 - C0 - 210/148/12 - PB - DID1593174